THE LITTLE BOOK OF
HOLIDAY LAW

URSULA FURI-PERRY

Cover design by Andrew Alcala/ABA Publishing.

The materials contained herein represent the opinions of the authors and/or the editors, and should not be construed to be the views or opinions of the law firms or companies with whom such persons are in partnership with, associated with, or employed by, nor of the American Bar Association or ABA Publishing unless adopted pursuant to the bylaws of the Association.

Nothing contained in this book is to be considered as the rendering of legal advice for specific cases, and readers are responsible for obtaining such advice from their own legal counsel. This book is intended for educational and informational purposes only.

© 2013 American Bar Association. All rights reserved.

No part of this publication may be reproduced, stored in a retrieval system, or transmitted in any form or by any means, electronic, mechanical, photocopying, recording, or otherwise, without the prior written permission of the publisher. For permission contact the ABA Copyrights & Contracts Department, copyright@americanbar.org, or complete the online form at http://www.americanbar.org/utility/reprint.html.

Printed in the United States of America.

17 16 15 14 13 5 4 3 2 1

Library of Congress Cataloging-in-Publication data is on file.

ISBN: 978-1-62722-417-8

Discounts are available for books ordered in bulk. Special consideration is given to state bars, CLE programs, and other bar-related organizations. Inquire at Book Publishing, ABA Publishing, American Bar Association, 321 N. Clark Street, Chicago, Illinois 60654-7598.

www.ShopABA.org

Table of Contents

3   **Chapter One**
January
The Establishment Clause and Holiday Law, Part I: Public Displays of Religious Holiday Items

13   **Chapter Two**
February
The Establishment Clause and Holiday Law, Part II: Public Schools and Holiday Celebrations

21   Holiday Humor
HOLIDAY MEANING

25   **Chapter Three**
March
Holidays and Family Law: Custody and Visitation Issues during Holidays

39   **Chapter Four**
April
Good Friday: Constitutional under the Establishment Clause?

43   Holiday Humor
APRIL FOOLS!

47   **Chapter Five**
May
A History of Law Day

54   Holiday Humor
HAPPY BELATED LAW DAY!

59 Chapter Six
June
Holidays and Labor Law: Paid and Unpaid
Holidays under Federal and State Labor Laws

69 Chapter Seven
July
Holidays and Court Procedures

77 Chapter Eight
August
Holidays and Business Law: The Effect of
Holidays on Business Filings and Acts

81 Chapter Nine
September
Official State and Local Holidays, from Secular
to Religious

87 Chapter Ten
October
Scary Cases: Halloween Pranks Gone Bad

99 Holiday Humor
HAL-LAW-EEN WOULD BE REALLY SCARY!

105 Chapter Eleven
November
A History of Blue Laws

113 Holiday Humor
AT THE FIRM FOR THE HOLIDAYS

117 Chapter Twelve
December
Holiday Party Liability: Cases on Social Host Liability, Office Party Suits, and More

123 Holiday Humor
A LITTLE HUMOR: HOLIDAY OFFICE PARTY SUGGESTIONS—NOT!

127 Index

132 About the Author

THE LITTLE BOOK OF

HOLIDAY LAW

Chapter One

January
The Establishment Clause and Holiday Law, Part I: Public Displays of Religious Holiday Items

As early as middle school, American children learn about the doctrine of separation of church and state, recognized and embedded in our legal system. The courts, however, have long concluded that total separation is impossible. Instead, the courts have employed various tests—which will be discussed in the next two chapters—to determine whether various situations, from city holiday displays to holiday celebrations in schools, violate First Amendment freedoms.

This chapter discusses a question that becomes visible around the holiday season each year: May local or state governments erect holiday displays on public property? The answer is a resounding yes. But may those displays include religious holiday items, such as a crèche (nativity scene) or a menorah? Yes, with qualification, the courts have ruled; overall, they may be displayed so long as they are in the company of secular symbols, like a Christmas tree, a holiday banner, or a figure of Santa Claus. As explained by the authors of a relevant article,

Furthermore, in areas deemed to be a public forum for free expression, local governments must allow private religious expression, but may prohibit persons from placing unattended displays there or adopt other policies governing how such displays will be handled (*i.e.*, size, length of display, safety of proposed location and installation, etc.).[1]

Two different clauses of the First Amendment are implicated by local and state government holiday displays. First, there is the Establishment Clause, which works to forbid government speech that would endorse religion.

To be held constitutional under the *Lemon* test, a challenged governmental action must 1) have a secular purpose; 2) have as its primary effect neither the advancement nor the inhibition of religion; and 3) not create excessive government entanglement with religion. Challenged conduct that does not meet all three criteria will be deemed to be unconstitutional under the Establishment Clause. A challenge to a government-sponsored holiday display would be analyzed under these criteria.[2]

Second, there is the Free Exercise Clause, which serves to protect private speech, including speech that endorses religion.

The local government's ability to control or limit private speech or expression is determined according to the location and context of the expression. The conditions that the

---

1. Susan Trevarthen & Johanna Lundgren, *Merry Litigation and Happy Attorneys' Fees: Holiday Displays on Downtown Public Property*, 85 FLA. B.J. 19, at 19 (Dec. 2011).
2. *Id.* at 22.

January—Public Displays of Religious Holiday Items

local government may place on expression in a public place depend on whether that place is deemed to be a "public forum" for free expression. Free speech rights are most extensive in a public forum, where governmental regulations of the content of expression are subject to "strict scrutiny" analysis, meaning that they must be narrowly drawn to serve a compelling governmental interest.[3]

The authors explain the various classifications of fora in First Amendment contexts:

- There is the traditional public forum, which is public property that "by its very nature is the type of property that has historically been held in trust for the use of the public and has traditionally been used for purposes of assembly, communication of thoughts, and discussion of public questions."[4] Some examples include city streets and sidewalks, along with public parks.[5]
- There is the designated public forum, which offers the same level of protection and includes "public property that the government has opened for public use as a place for expressive activity, although not traditionally used for such purposes."[6] Some examples include school board meeting rooms and state college classrooms.[7]
- There is the limited public forum, which is public property that the government has designated for only certain types of activities. When the state establishes a limited public forum,

---

3. *Id.* at 19.
4. *Id.*
5. *Id.*
6. *Id.* at 20.
7. *Id.*

it is not required to allow persons to engage in every type of speech and may be justified in reserving the forum for certain groups. However, any restrictions must not discriminate against speech based on its viewpoint and must be reasonable in light of the purpose served by the forum.[8]
- Finally, there is the nonpublic forum, which includes "any other public property that has not been traditionally used for or designated for use as a forum for expressive activity," such as an elevated sidewalk extending from a U.S. Postal Service office to the public sidewalk.[9]

To understand the jurisprudence behind holiday displays and the Free Exercise and Establishment clauses, three key decisions must be examined.

The first, *Lynch v. Donnelly*, involved an annual holiday display in the city of Pawtucket, Rhode Island, in a park owned by a nonprofit organization and located in the city's shopping district. The display included a Santa Claus house, reindeer, candy-striped poles, a Christmas tree, carolers and other characters, colored lights, a banner, and a crèche with traditional religious figures. Residents and members of the American Civil Liberties Union (ACLU) brought suit against the city, claiming that the inclusion of the crèche violated the Establishment Clause.[10] The federal district court held for the plaintiffs, and the appellate court affirmed.

On appeal, the U.S. Supreme Court first recognized that total separation of church and state is impossible, and that this line of jurisprudence requires fact-by-fact application. "In every Establishment Clause case, we must reconcile the inescapable tension

---

8. *Id.*
9. *Id.*
10. Lynch v. Donnelly, 465 U.S. 668 (1984).

January—Public Displays of Religious Holiday Items

between the objective of preventing unnecessary intrusion of either the church or the state upon the other, and the reality that, as the Court has so often noted, total separation of the two is not possible."[11]

The high Court then gave several examples that made it "clear that Government has long recognized—indeed it has subsidized—holidays with religious significance."[12] Among those examples were:

- the phrase "In God We Trust" printed on money;
- the phrase "One Nation Under God" as part of the Pledge of Allegiance;
- masterpieces with religious messages housed in the National Gallery;
- Congress's provisions for chapels in the Capitol for religious worship and meditation;
- proclamations of a National Day of Prayer, along with recognition of various religious "heritage weeks."[13]

The history, the high Court stated, helped explain why the Court has declined to take an absolutist view of the Establishment Clause, and why each case and each inquiry called for line drawing.[14]

As for the Pawtucket holiday display, the high Court held that the city did not violate the Establishment Clause and it reversed the lower courts' holdings. The Court noted:

> When viewed in the proper context of the Christmas Holiday season, it is apparent that, on this record, there is insufficient evidence to establish that the inclusion of the crèche is a

---

11. *Id.* at 672.
12. *Id.* at 676.
13. *Id.* at 676–77.
14. *Id.* at 678–79.

purposeful or surreptitious effort to express some kind of subtle governmental advocacy of a particular religious message. In a pluralistic society a variety of motives and purposes are implicated. The City, like the Congresses and Presidents, however, has principally taken note of a significant historical religious event long celebrated in the Western World. The crèche in the display depicts the historical origins of this traditional event long recognized as a National Holiday.[15]

Just five years later, the case of *County of Allegheny v. ACLU, Greater Pittsburgh Chapter*, found its way to the Supreme Court. That case involved two instances that the plaintiffs alleged violated the Establishment Clause. In the first, a crèche was situated in the Allegheny County Courthouse, along with a banner exclaiming "In Excelsius Deo!" or "Glory to God in the Highest!" In the second, situated outside the City-County Building located in Pittsburgh, Pennsylvania, were a Hanukah menorah, a decorated Christmas tree, and a sign stating, "During this holiday season, the city of Pittsburgh salutes liberty. Let these festive lights remind us that we are keepers of the flame of liberty and our legacy of freedom."[16]

---

15. *Id.* at 680.
16. County of Allegheny v. ACLU, Greater Pittsburgh Chapter, 492 U.S. 573 (1989).

January—Public Displays of Religious Holiday Items

> ### Holiday Fast Facts—Valentine's Day
>
> Each year, one billion Valentine cards are given in the United States.[1] Teachers get the most cards, while children are second.[2] One-fifth of the world's chocolate and cocoa is eaten by Americans.[3]
>
> ---
>
> 1. Peter & Connie Roop, Let's Celebrate Valentine's Day 17 (1999).
> 2. *Id.*
> 3. *Id.* at 11.

The high Court struck down the first display, noting that the crèche stood alone and no other (secular) decorations served to detract from its religious purposes. "There is no doubt, of course, that the crèche itself is capable of communicating a religious message," it noted.[17] "Indeed, the crèche in this lawsuit uses words, as well as the picture of the Nativity scene, to make its religious meaning unmistakably clear."[18]

The Court rejected the county's argument that it was allowed to display the crèche simply because Christmas was a national holiday.

> This argument obviously proves too much. It would allow the celebration of the Eucharist inside a courthouse on Christmas Eve. . . . The government may acknowledge Christmas as a cultural phenomenon, but under the First Amendment it may not observe it as a Christian holy day by suggesting that people praise God for the birth of Jesus.[19]

---

17. *Id.* at 598.
18. *Id.*
19. *Id.* at 601.

While the government may celebrate Christmas, the County of Allegheny decided to do so in such a manner as to endorse Christian doctrine, the Court held.[20]

The Court reached a different opinion regarding the second display, which was provided in three separate opinions by a rather splintered majority. The opinions emphasized that the second display did not have the effect of endorsing religion, but rather showed a more secular message.[21]

In her opinion, however, Justice O'Connor noted her view that the Court's upholding of the display didn't hinge upon whether it included symbols from both Hanukah and Christmas. "If the City celebrates both Christmas and Chanukah as religious holidays, then it violates the Establishment Clause,"[22] she cautioned. She elaborated as follows:

> The simultaneous endorsement of Judaism and Christianity is no less constitutionally infirm than the endorsement of Christianity alone. . . . Conversely, if the city celebrates both Christmas and Chanukah as secular holidays, then its conduct is beyond the reach of the Establishment Clause. Because government may celebrate Christmas as a secular holiday, it follows that government may also acknowledge Chanukah as a secular holiday.[23]

Thus, the question under the Establishment Clause, Justice O'Connor noted, is whether the combined display had the effect of endorsing several religions—or merely acknowledging that those religions are all part of the same winter-holiday season.[24]

---

20. *Id.*
21. *See Id.* at 616–19 and 632.
22. *Id.* at 614–15.
23. *Id.* at 615.
24. *Id.* at 616.

January—Public Displays of Religious Holiday Items

"In these circumstances, then, the combination of the tree and menorah communicates not a simultaneous endorsement of both the Christian and Jewish faiths, but instead a secular celebration of Christmas coupled with an acknowledgment of Chanukah as a contemporaneous alternative tradition,"[25] she concluded.

Following these two landmark Supreme Court cases, the Third Circuit Court of Appeals issued its own decision in a similar case in 1999. The case, *ACLU of New Jersey v. Schundler*, involved plaintiffs who sought declaratory and injunctive relief over Jersey City's maintenance of a holiday display on city hall plaza, the original version of which included a crèche and a menorah, both owned by the city. Through the proceedings, the federal district court granted the plaintiffs' request for an injunction, and also enjoined the city from erecting any substantially similar display on property it owned.

In the meantime, the city erected a new display. That display included a crèche, a menorah, Kwanzaa symbols, and a Christmas tree, along with a sign that stated, "Through this display and others throughout the year, the City of Jersey City is pleased to celebrate the diverse cultural and ethnic heritages of its people." The plaintiffs moved for an injunction, claiming the modified display was constitutionally objectionable. The district court once again agreed.

The federal appeals court, however, disagreed and reversed. The court noted that the modified display was indistinguishable from the display in the *Lynch* case. "Reasonably viewed, none of these displays conveyed a message of government endorsement of Christianity, Judaism, or of religion in general," the court held, but rather sent a message of pluralism and endorsed the freedom to choose one's own beliefs.[26]

---

25. *Id.* at 617–18.
26. *Id.* at 107.

Chapter Two

February
The Establishment Clause and Holiday Law, Part II: Public Schools and Holiday Celebrations

As one article explains, the Supreme Court of the United States has not yet directly addressed the constitutionality of holiday displays in public schools, but school officials should be cautious in this area.

> First, any religious display that bears the imprimatur of public school officials will be suspect. Thus, even the display of a Christmas tree, with or without religious symbols such as angels, in a school hallway or a classroom may be suspect because the tree arguably promotes a particular religion. Focusing on one religion, such as showing only videotapes on the Christian holidays of Christmas and Easter to explain the real purpose of these holidays, will run afoul of the Establishment Clause. Second, diluting the impact of a religious message with other clearly secular content may be sufficient to overcome an Establishment Clause challenge. As suggested by the cases above, including a wide range of ethnic and religious symbols in a display may pass constitutional

muster as furtherance of diversity. Including religious music during public school choir holiday concerts, and even performing that music at religious sites, can be considered a matter of permissible teacher and/or school discretion, as long as non–religious music and sites are also selected.[1]

Of course, as with the cases in the previous chapter regarding holiday displays on public property, "[m]uch of the difficulty in determining permissible governmental involvement with holiday displays results from both the nature of the holiday season and the holiday displays themselves," notes another author. "The holiday season traditionally has been considered a time of religious celebration."[2]

Over time, however, the secular aspects of the holiday seasons and holiday symbols have commingled with the religious aspects, so that the seasons and symbols have become equivocal in their true meaning and purpose. Further, the many symbols associated with the holiday season incorporate at once varying degrees of historical, religious, and popular significance. The pervasive ambiguity of these symbols significantly affects substantive establishment clause analysis and has caused the Supreme Court to use a distinct case-by-case approach in deciding holiday display cases.[3]

"It is difficult to imagine walking into an elementary school after Thanksgiving and not seeing evidence of the impending Christmas holiday," notes another author.[4]

---

1. Ralph D. Mawdsley & Charles J. Russo, *Religious Holiday Celebrations in Public Schools: What Is Permissible and What Is Prohibited?*, WEST'S EDUC. L. REP. 3 (Dec. 18, 2003).
2. Gregory J. Blackburn, Government, *The Holiday Season, and the Establishment Clause: A Perspective on the Issues*, 20 STETSON L. REV. 217 (1990).
3. *Id.* at 217–18.
4. John M. Hartenstein, *A Christmas Issue: Christian Holiday Celebration in the Public Elementary Schools Is an Establishment of Religion,*

February—Public Schools and Holiday Celebrations

Because the Supreme Court has prohibited religious prayer in public schools, most schools try to avoid conveying any explicit Christian message in their holiday observances. Diversity of ethnicity and religious practice in many urban areas has also led some schools to include other holiday observances in their "winter holiday" celebrations. But Christmas is so widely accepted and entrenched in American culture that its religious origins and content are usually overlooked, and few would seriously consider altogether proscribing Christmas observances in public elementary schools.[5]

In the development of freedom-of-religion jurisprudence, the Supreme Court has been keenly aware of the precarious situation of schoolchildren who are compelled by the state to tolerate whatever messages the state wishes to communicate in its schools. The Court's concern for protecting impressionable young minds has its roots in the earliest First Amendment cases, including those not directly interpreting the Establishment Clause. It echoes concerns of the founding fathers—concerns that have been re-echoed in university, public school, parochial school, and even nonschool Establishment Clause cases, irrespective of outcome.[6]

Thus, in any First Amendment inquiry in the elementary school context, the special susceptibility of young children must be taken into account. It is a distinct issue that sharpens any test: state action that passes constitutional scrutiny when it affects the general public can constitute impermissible religious indoctrination when it takes place in an elementary school.[7]

---

80 CAL. L. REV. 981 (1992).
5. *Id.*
6. *Id.* at 1004.
7. *Id.* at 1005–06.

But can there be such a thing as "too little Christianity" in public school holiday celebrations? One case discussed exactly that issue. The case involved attendance at a winter holiday program at an elementary school. One of the plaintiffs complained that he was barred from participating as a volunteer lunchroom chaperone because he was a youth pastor at a Christian church, while the other (a parent who attended the celebration with his school children) complained that there were no Christian symbols at the holiday program he attended.[8]

According to the plaintiffs, the school displayed a table with a menorah and a Kwanzaa candelabra, along with books about Kwanzaa and Hanukah and a general book on celebrations. The parent also complained that the program was "not Christian enough" and included a song spoofing Christmas—a song, sung to the tune of a Christian hymn, which told the story of children who go shopping with their grandmother and are forgotten inside a mall, where they proceed to have fun and roam around.

The federal court rejected the plaintiffs' argument that we somehow tally up points for religious symbols versus secular symbols. "We also choose not to decide how many candy canes offset one Jesus. The fact is there were symbols of Christmas displayed and the song program included Christmas carols. No particular faith was preferred at the expense of others, and a reasonable observer would not so conclude."[9]

And as for that supposed song parody? The court declined to say it demonstrated hostility towards Christianity. "We recognize that Christmas is a time of serious commemoration, but it is also a festive time," the court explained. "This song is about nothing

---

[8]. Sechler v. State Coll. Area Sch. Dist., 121 F. Supp. 2d 439 (M.D. Pa. 2000).
[9]. *Id.* at 451.

February—Public Schools and Holiday Celebrations

more than children having fun during the Christmas season, and a reasonable observer would not find that offensive."[10]

In another case, a federal district court ruled that a school district policy requiring classrooms to display and maintain calendars that depicted various national, ethnic, and religious holidays and permitting seasonal displays was constitutional.[11] (The court remarked: "The Christmas season brings with it not only sidewalk Santas, mercantile mania, and endless reruns of *It's a Wonderful Life* and *Miracle on 34th Street*, but also a staple of constitutional litigation testing the limits to which governmental or public bodies may legally join the festivities.")[12]

In that case, parents of students and a resident brought suit against the school board, claiming violations of the First and Fourteenth Amendments. The use of the calendars in question was mandated by the school board in elementary and middle schools and optional in high schools, while the seasonal displays in question were permissible but not required in any school. The policy also mandated that the calendars be used in conjunction with books and resource materials, and each teacher was given descriptions of holidays to be used as an educational resource.

Applying the *Lemon* test, the court concluded that the calendars and seasonal displays did not violate the Establishment Clause. "Given the emphasis [the school board policy] places on religious diversity, there is simply no basis for concluding that it endorses any particular religion," the court noted.[13] It went on to explain:

> Nor can it be said to favor religion over non-religion. The language of the policy completely disclaims any such intent:

---

10. *Id.* at 452.
11. Clever v. Cherry Hill Twp. Bd. of Educ., 838 F. Supp. 929 (D. N.J. 1993).
12. *Id.* at 931.
13. *Id.* at 940.

The Little Book of Holiday Law

"Schools may teach about but not promote religion." To the extent the record reflects the actual implementation of that policy, the calendars for November and December, which celebrate a wide variety of religious and secular holidays, confirm that its intent is being fairly implemented.[14]

Holiday Fast Facts—Presidents' Day

Presidents' Day honors two presidents: George Washington and Abraham Lincoln. Their birthdays used to be celebrated separately; because they are both in February, a joint holiday was proposed and became a legal holiday in most states.[1]

---

1. CASS R. SANDAK, PATRIOTIC HOLIDAYS 16–20 (1990).

A holiday that is a kid favorite, of course, is Halloween—but not everyone enjoys the witches' brew. In one case, the parent of a student filed suit against the school system, claiming that the depiction of cauldrons, witches, and brooms in elementary school decorations were religious symbols and therefore violated the Establishment Clause.[15]

The court disagreed.

> [T]here is no doubt that the Halloween festivities and decorations serve a secular purpose. According to the school principal, the costumes and decorations serve to make Halloween a fun day for students and serve an educational

---

14. *Id.*
15. Guyer v. Sch. Bd. of Alachua County, 634 So. 2d 806 (Dist. Ct. of App. Fla., 1994).

February—Public Schools and Holiday Celebrations

purpose by enriching their educational background and cultural awareness. The record also reflects that this cultural celebration enhances a sense of community. In addition, the Halloween festivities and decorations do not foster any excessive entanglement between government and religion.[16]

"The determinative question is not whether the witch, cauldron, and broom are capable of communicating a religious message to some people. . . . What is determinative is the context in which these symbols are displayed," the court continued.[17]

The First Amendment does not prohibit practices which by any realistic measure create none of the dangers which it is designed to prevent and which do not directly or substantially involve the state in religious exercises or in the favoring of religion as to have meaningful and practical impact. It is of course true that great consequences can grow from small beginnings, but the measure of constitutional adjudication is the ability and willingness to distinguish between real threat and mere shadow. Witches, cauldrons, and brooms in the context of a school Halloween celebration appear to be nothing more than a mere "shadow," if that, in the realm of establishment clause jurisprudence.[18]

Another case discussed a school policy that required students to obtain prior approval of the school superintendent before they could distribute any written materials on school grounds. In that case, a student wished to distribute invitations to a church party as an alternative to Halloween trick-or-treating, but the principal

---
16. *Id.* at 808.
17. *Id.*
18. *Id.* at 809.

told the student that she could not distribute religious materials in school and that he discarded her invitations.[19]

The student's parent sued the school, claiming that the school's policy constituted content-based prior restraint in violation of the First Amendment to the U.S. Constitution. Although the student had transferred to a private school, the court noted that the plaintiff had standing to sue, as she remained a resident of the state and was entitled to a free state education.[20]

On the First Amendment claims, the federal court sided with the plaintiff, noting that the school has failed to show that the religious speech it sought to prevent would materially and substantially interfere with school operations or the rights of others.[21]

"Indeed, free speech protection as contemplated by the First Amendment frequently experiences its vitality from controversy. Undisruptive controversy ought not to be unnecessarily harnessed. Indeed, it is frequently viewed as a teaching tool."[22] The court granted the plaintiff's request for a permanent injunction against enforcement of the school policy.

---

19. Johnston-Loehner v. O'Brien, 859 F. Supp. 574 (M.D. Fla. 1994).
20. *Id.* at 578.
21. *Id.* at 581.
22. *Id.*

February—Public Schools and Holiday Celebrations

HOLIDAY MEANING

By Vincent P. Fornias

Gift	From Spouse	From Former Spouse	From Office Assistant	From Client
Gold	Love	Regrets	Graft	Results
Silver	Appreciation	Acceptable alimony	Too many raises	Half-interest in S. African mine
Tupperware ®	Honeymoon's over	Depends on whether it's been through the rinse cycle	Need a raise—badly	Your bill will be audited
Booze	Warning about January bills	Cirrhosis wish	Confiscate the holiday party video!	In D.W.I. conviction denial
A wad of unmarked currency	That Junior League trip made a stop in Guatemala	Entrapment attempt	She won the office bowl pool	Imminent "IOLTA" Hall of Fame status
Underwear	New or used?	Whose?	Lawsuit	Disbarment
E-mail greeting	Found another love	www.insults.com went free	Looking for other employment	Found another lawyer
Fruit basket	Your Metamucil ain't working	How rotten?	Regifting	Uses lots of your competitors

Holiday Humor

21

The Little Book of Holiday Law

Gift	From Spouse	From Former Spouse	From Office Assistant	From Client
Puppy	Needs new carpeting	Hates your present spouse	Got night job at SPCA	Owns landscape business
Python	Hated the Tupperware ®	How fast is the puppy?	Two weeks' notice	Got his year-end bill

Reprinted from the Louisiana Bar Journal (December 2005/January 2006). Copyright © 2005 by Louisiana State Bar Association; Vincent P. Fornias.

Chapter Three

March
Holidays and Family Law: Custody and Visitation Issues during Holidays

Family law practitioners know that one of the points of contention in divorce proceedings might be issues with holiday time, the time spent by each parent with his or her child or children during holidays. Two practitioners, writing in a practical guide for attorneys, offer the following advice:

> Be sure to consult with the client to determine what religious holidays are observed by the family, if any. Keep in mind that some families observe the religious holidays of more than one faith. Watch out for holidays which fall within school vacations. For example, if Easter may fall within the child's spring vacation, giving Easter to one parent and the spring vacation to the other may generate needless ambiguities and conflicts. If a particular holiday may involve an extended weekend (Ex: Labor Day Weekend) it may be advisable to

The Little Book of Holiday Law

specify whether the agreement refers to the single day or the entire weekend.[1]

The following is an example of a sample parenting plan regarding holiday time, which might just help avoid some of the related disputes:

Comprehensive Schedule for Alternating Holidays and Vacations[2]

Contact With Primary Parent During Summer Parenting Time:

During the children's summertime parenting time with the [Husband/Wife],except for a period of two consecutive weeks when the [Husband/Wife]'s time with the children shall be uninterrupted, the [Wife/Husband] shall have the right to have such contact and access with the children as the [Husband/Wife] had during the regular school term.

Division of Christmas Holiday:

On a schedule of alternating years, either the Husband or the Wife will have the children on Christmas Eve and the other party will have the children on Christmas Day. Where travel to the Husband's place of abode is involved, the Wife is to deliver the children and the Husband will return them.

---

1. 20 Colo. Prac., Family Law & Practice § 41:25 (2d ed.), article by Frank L. McGuane, Jr, Kathleen A. Hogan.
2. *Id.*

March—Holidays and Family Law

Parenting Time During Christmas Vacation:

The [Husband/Wife] shall each have parenting time for a period of one week during the child's Christmas school vacation, with said week to [(begin at [specification of time period 1] o'clock [a.m./p.m.] on the first day that school recesses and to end at [specification of time period 2] o'clock [a.m./p.m.] seven days later.)/(begin at [specification of time period 1] o'clock [a.m./p.m.] on the day seven days prior to the date school reconvenes and to end at [specification of time period 2] o'clock [a.m./p.m.] on the day before school is to reconvene.)]

Alternation of Thanksgiving and Christmas:

The parties will alternate having the child for the Thanksgiving and Christmas holidays.

In [identification of year] and subsequent odd-numbered years the Wife will have the child for Thanksgiving [Day/Weekend] and the Husband will have the child on Christmas Eve and up until 11:00 a.m. on Christmas Day. In [identification of year] and subsequent even-numbered years, the Husband will have the child for Thanksgiving [Day/Weekend] and the Wife will have him on Christmas Eve and up until 11:00 a.m. on Christmas Day. The Husband will have the child from 11:00 a.m. on Christmas Day until 11:00 a.m. the following day.

The Little Book of Holiday Law

Adoption of School Schedule for Parenting Time Purposes:

For purposes of parenting time arrangements under this Agreement, and the designation of school break and vacation times, the parties shall immediately adopt the schedule of the [name of public school] Public School system, notwithstanding that the child has not yet started school, so that such time blocks may be used as reference points.

Alternation of Holidays and Vacations:
The holiday parenting time schedule shall be as follows:

a. The parties shall alternate the following holidays: Memorial Day and Labor Day, so that if the Husband has the child for Labor Day in an odd-numbered year, the Wife will have the child for Memorial Day, and in the following even-numbered year Labor Day will be with the Wife and Memorial Day with the Husband. In the event that Easter or Presidents' Day is not included in one of the longer school breaks dealt with below, those holidays shall also be alternated as set forth herein. In the event that any of the above-referenced holidays involves a 3-day weekend, the parent entitled to have the child for the holiday shall have the entire weekend.
b. Thanksgiving, from Wednesday after school until Monday morning, shall be with the Husband in odd-numbered years and with the Wife in even-numbered years.
c. Christmas shall be with the Wife in odd-numbered years and with the Husband in even numbered years. For purposes of this Agreement, Christmas shall consist of the entire school holiday. The parties understand that this will likely also

March—Holidays and Family Law

include the New Years holiday so no separate arrangement is made for that holiday.

d. Apart from the foregoing, the parties will alternate the Winter and Spring school recesses. Winter recess will be with the Husband in odd-numbered years and with the Wife in even-numbered years. Spring recess will be with the Wife in odd-numbered years and with the Husband in even-numbered years. The party who has the child for a school vacation shall be entitled to take the child on vacation for the entire holiday. However, if he or she elects to remain in the area the other parent shall be entitled to mid-week parenting time as set forth in [designation of exhibit].

e. In addition to the foregoing, the Husband shall have the child with him on Father's Day, on the Husband's birthday, and on the paternal grandmother's birthday. The child shall be with the Wife on Mother's Day, on the Wife's birthday, and on the maternal grandparents' birthdays.

f. Apart from the parenting time described above, the Husband shall have the child for the month of July and the Wife shall have the child for the month of August. The parent who does not have the child for the month in question shall be entitled to alternating weekends with the child as described above, unless the child and parent will be staying outside [name of state] during that entire period.

g. In the event there is a conflict between the regular parenting time schedule described in Paragraph [number of paragraph] and the holiday, vacation and birthday schedules referred to in Paragraphs [number of paragraphs], the holiday, vacation or birthday schedule shall prevail.

The Little Book of Holiday Law

With regard to the parenting time schedule, the parties agree to maintain flexibility to accommodate the business and personal commitments of each.

Alternation of Jewish Holy Days:

With respect to Passover and Rosh Hashanah, each party shall have the right to be with the children for one of the first two days of each holiday every year; and if one party is with the children for the first day of one of those two holidays, the other party shall have the right to be with the child for the first day of the other holiday in the same year. In odd numbered years, the Wife shall have the right to be with the children for the first night of Passover and the second night of Rosh Hashanah, and the Husband shall have the right to be with the children for the first night of Passover and the second night of Rosh Hashanah. In even numbered years, the Husband shall have the right to be with the children on the first night of Passover and the second night of Rosh Hashanah, and the Wife shall have the right to be with the children on the second night of Passover and the first night of Rosh Hashanah.

Each party shall have the right to be with the children at some time during Chanukah each year, and they shall make mutually convenient arrangements for such holiday celebration.

Alternation of Thanksgiving and Easter:

On a schedule of alternating years, one party is to have the children Thanksgiving Day and the other party is to have them Easter Day.

March—Holidays and Family Law

School Vacation Parenting Time:

In any extended recesses from school, such as a winter or spring break or summer vacation, the Husband shall have the option of having the children for a week. Both the Husband and the Wife agree to show consideration for and defer to reasonable plans made for or by the children that involve travel, camp, educational or similar commitments during recess periods and that may otherwise interfere with home residence or parenting time.

Child's Birthday:

Both parties shall have reasonable access and opportunity to celebrate with their child on the occasion of each child's birthday. OR The child shall spend his/her birthday with the Mother in even numbered years and with the Father in odd numbered years. OR The child shall spend their actual birthdays with the parent who is scheduled to care for them under the routine parenting schedule. The parties shall alternate planning and hosting the child's birthday party with each parent in charge of the party for the child's friends and peers for one of the children each year. Each parent shall advise the other of the date, time and location of the party he or she is planning as much in advance as possible and shall offer the other parent the opportunity to attend the party, only in the event that the parenting coordinator does not feel that it would be an uncomfortable situation for the child. Nothing herein shall preclude either parent, in any year, from arranging any informal birthday observances he or she wishes during his or her time with the child.

The Little Book of Holiday Law

Allocation of Weekends, Holiday Weekends and Vacations:

h. The Husband shall have parenting time with the child alternate weekends from Friday evening to Sunday evening, and for four weeks during the year, not necessarily consecutive.
i. The Husband shall have the child for each of the federally recognized 3-day holiday weekends except July 4th, which will be spent with the Wife.
j. In the event that the regular schedule of alternating weekends conflicts with the holiday weekend schedule, the holiday schedule will prevail, but the parties will exchange weekends so that the party who does not have the child for the holiday weekend will have the child for the weekend preceding or the weekend following the holiday.

Comprehensive Alternating Holiday Schedule:

Each year the Wife will have the child on the weekend that includes Mother's Day and the Husband will have the child on the weekend that includes Father's Day.

In even numbered years, the Husband shall have the child on the following holidays:
—Palm Sunday
—Labor Day Weekend (3-day weekend from Friday at 6:00 p.m. to Monday at 6:00 p.m.);
—Thanksgiving (4-day weekend from Wednesday at 6:00 p.m. through Sunday at 6:00 p.m.);
—New Years (6-day block commencing December 28 at 6:00 p.m. through January 3 at 6:00 p.m., including New Year's Eve and New Year's Day);

March—Holidays and Family Law

In even numbered years, the Wife shall have the child on the following holidays:
 —Presidents' Day Weekend (3-day weekend from Friday at 6:00 p.m. through Monday at 6:00 p.m.)
 —Easter Sunday;
 —Memorial Day Weekend (3-day weekend from Friday at 6:00 p.m. through Monday at 6:00 p.m.);
 —Christmas (6-day block from December 22 at 6:00 p.m. through December 28 at 6:00 p.m., including Christmas Eve and Christmas Day).

In odd numbered years, the above schedules will be reversed. The child's birthday will be alternated between the parties.

To the extent that a full weekend holiday disrupts the routine parenting time schedule, the parties agree to confer and attempt to accommodate one another. To the extent that a party is deprived of a regular weekend, compensating time shall be allowed at a later date if no immediate adjustment is possible.

Comprehensive Schedule for Alternating Holidays, Vacations and Special Days:

xi. The children shall be with their father from 9 o'clock in the morning on Easter Day and Labor Day, [list of holidays 1] and shall similarly be with the mother on Memorial Day and Thanksgiving Day, [list of holidays 2]. Thereafter, the parents will alternate the foregoing holidays. If the day after any such holiday is a day on which the other parent would normally have the children, they shall be returned to that parent by 9 o'clock in the morning.

The Little Book of Holiday Law

xii. The children shall be with the father from 9 o'clock in the morning on Christmas Eve day through Christmas Eve, [date of holiday 1] until 10 o'clock in the morning on Christmas Day, at which time they will be with their mother for the remainder of Christmas Day, [date of holiday 2]. Thereafter the parents will alternate Christmas Eve and Christmas Day in the foregoing manner. If the day after Christmas is a day on which the other parent would normally have the children, they shall be returned to that parent by 9 o'clock in the morning.
   a. Birthdays: The children shall be with the father from 9 o'clock in the morning on [date of birthday 1], and with the mother from 9 o'clock in the morning on [date of birthday 2]. Thereafter the parents will alternate the children's birthdays. If the day after the birthday is a day on which the other parent would normally have the children, they shall be returned to that parent by 9 o'clock in the morning.
   b. During the summer of [identification of year], the children shall spend the month of July with the mother and the month of August with the father.

Thereafter, the children will alternate the summer vacation schedule in the foregoing manner.

Holiday and School Vacation Parenting Time Schedule: The holiday parenting time schedule shall be as follows:

m. The parties shall alternate the following holidays: New Year's Day, Presidents' Day, Easter, Memorial Day, July 4 and Labor Day, so that if the Husband has the child for New Year's Day in an odd-numbered year, the Wife will have the child for

March—Holidays and Family Law

Presidents' Day, and in the following even-numbered year New Year's Day will be with the Wife and Presidents' Day with the Husband.

n. Thanksgiving will be with the Husband in odd-numbered years and with the Wife in even-numbered years.

o. Christmas will be alternated so that in odd-numbered years the child will be with the Wife from 5:00 p.m. on December 24 until noon on December 25, and with the Husband from noon on December 25. In even-numbered years, the child will be with the Husband from 5:00 p.m. on December 24 until noon on December 25, and with the Wife from noon on December 25.

p. Apart from the foregoing the parties will split the Christmas recess. In addition, the parties will alternate the Winter and Spring school recesses. Winter recess will be with the Husband in odd-numbered years and with the Wife in even-numbered years. Spring recess will be with the Wife in odd-numbered years and with the Husband in even-numbered years. The Husband will use his best efforts to have his vacations from employment coincide with the child's school vacations.

The Little Book of Holiday Law

> ### Holiday Fast Facts—St. Patrick's Day
>
> The first St. Patrick's Day celebration on record was organized in Boston in 1737. Although the day is celebrated widely across the United States on March 17 of each year, it is actually a legal holiday in Suffolk County, where Boston is located, celebrated alongside Evacuation Day.[1]
>
> ---
>
> 1. *See* http://www.sec.state.ma.us/cis/cishol/holidx.htm.

Comprehensive Schedule for Alternating Holidays and Vacations:

The following holidays and holiday periods shall be alternated between the Husband and Wife with the child: Presidents' Day, Easter Week, Memorial Day Weekend, Independence Day, Labor Day Weekend, Columbus Day, Thanksgiving Day and weekend, any other annual school holidays, and each party shall have one-half of the Christmas-New Year's holiday vacation, alternating the first and second half thereof on a yearly basis. In addition, each child's birthday shall be alternated between the Husband and the Wife, and the children shall spend Mother's Day and the mother's birthday with the mother and Father's Day and the father's birthday with the father. Regardless of what may be otherwise indicated by the general custody and parenting time schedule, the holiday and birthday schedule shall control over the regular physical custody and access schedule utilized by the parties.

Chapter Four

April
Good Friday: Constitutional under the Establishment Clause?

Good Friday, which is celebrated the Friday before Easter, is the day on which Christians commemorate the crucifixion of Jesus Christ. In recent years, the courts have grappled with the issue of Good Friday as a legal holiday, explains one author, who poses the question: Does its celebration as a legal holiday violate the Establishment Clause of the First Amendment?[1] "Because most of the circuit cases concerning the Good Friday holiday have been decided two to one, the majority in any circuit could easily shift, changing the law overnight."[2]

Two cases that occurred in the 1990s are of note. The first, *Cammack v. Waihee*, involved a Hawaii statute declaring Good Friday a legal holiday.[3] The U.S. Court of Appeals for the Ninth Circuit held that the statute was constitutional, as it would have violated the Establishment Clause only if it were prompted wholly by an

---

1. *See* Megan E. Kleinfelder, *Good Friday: Just Another Spring Holiday?*, 69 U. CIN. L. REV. 329 (2000).
2. *Id.* at 329.
3. Cammack v. Waihee, 932 F. 2d 765 (9th Cir. 1991).

impermissible purpose, and had no secular value. In this case, the court said, the legislative purpose behind enacting the statute was to create more legal holidays, which was a legitimate, secular purpose. The court had no issue with Hawaii choosing a spring holiday that happened to be a day of religious significance to Christians; it noted that Good Friday was also a popular day of shopping and recreational activities, and not just a day for religious observance.[4]

"There is nothing impermissible about considering for holiday status days on which many people choose to be absent from work for religious reasons," the court said. "That the state legislature was able to accomplish its secular purpose and at the same time accommodate the widespread religious practices of its citizenry is hardly a reason to invalidate the statute."[5]

In another case, *Metzl v. Leininger*, the Seventh Circuit struck down an Illinois statute that mandated public schools to close on Good Friday. The court in that case noted that Good Friday was a day of solemnity and religious observance by practicing Christians.[6] "[T]he challenged statute, given the unambiguously sectarian character of Good Friday, promotes one religion over others, and such a statute violates the [E]stablishment [C]lause unless it has a secular justification," evidence of which the court noted was not produced by the state.[7]

Two conflicting California cases have addressed the legality of the Good Friday holiday in the context of labor and employment law. The first, from 1976, affirmed an injunction against the governor from proclaiming Good Friday, between noon and 3 p.m., to be a holiday, also enjoining the state comptroller from paying state employees for time taken off work during that span. The court in

---

4. *Id.* at 777–78.
5. *Id.* at 777.
6. Metzl v. Leininger, 57 F. 3d 618 (7th Cir. 1995).
7. *Id.* at 622.

April—Good Friday

that case concluded that there was no evidence that Good Friday had become a secularized holiday, and that the trial court could correctly conclude that it was a wholly religious day.[8]

A year later, the California appellate court decided another Good Friday case, this one involving the contractual designation of the day as a paid holiday for a school district's classified employees. The court in that case held that the provision did not violate the Establishment Clause, because it was negotiated by the school employees' union as part of a wage and fringe benefit agreement—a negotiation in which the union was empowered to take part, the court noted.[9]

In 1999, three other cases of note were decided. The first, coming from the Sixth Circuit, involved a holiday closing schedule that was adopted by some courts in Kentucky. The district court case also addressed the issue of announcing the closings, which was done by way of posting signs around the courthouse that included the image of the crucifixion; the district judge enjoined the defendants from posting overtly religious signs, and that issue was not taken up on appeal.[10]

As for the issue of the closings themselves, they were upheld by the Sixth Circuit court. The court was not concerned with the religious significance of the Good Friday tradition; rather, it noted the day's secular purpose of providing a "break for their employees at that time of year, conveniently scheduled on a day of light activity and proximate to many families' vacations."[11] The court noted that many children were on school vacation during the week following Good Friday, prompting many families to start their vacation on

---

8. Mandel v. Hodges, 54 Cal. App. 3d 596 (1976).
9. California Sch. Employees Ass'n v. Sequoia Union High Sch. Dist., 67 Cal. App. 3d 157 (1977).
10. Ganzeier v. Middleton, 173 F. 3d 568 (6th Cir. 1999).
11. *Id.* at 574.

that day, and that courts and government offices do not expect a lot of activity on that day.[12]

Another 1999 case upheld an Indiana statute making Good Friday a legal holiday. Distinguishing the case from its previous decision in *Metzl*, the court noted that the legislature's intent in this case was to provide a spring holiday to state employees during a time span in which otherwise there would be no break for employees for over four months.[13] The court also noted that the statute did not violate the Establishment Clause simply because it made it easier for Christians to practice their religion; such benefit was merely "indirect, remote and incidental" to the holiday's secular purpose.[14]

The Fourth Circuit, meanwhile, also upheld the constitutionality of a Maryland statute that provided for public school closings on Good Friday and the Monday after Easter.[15] The school board defendant argued that such closings were necessary, as high rates of absenteeism on those days were causing disruption in the classroom and wasting limited educational resources. The court noted that, since all students (not just Christian students) were given Good Friday off, the school closings did not advance or endorse Christianity or religion in general.[16]

The U.S. Supreme Court has not ventured to accept a case that would definitively decide the fate of the Good Friday holiday. Until that happens, state and local governments (and schools and employers) are free to proscribe Good Friday as a spring holiday. And, hey, who doesn't love an extra day off?

---

12. *Id.*
13. Bridenbaugh v. O'Bannon, 185 F. 3d 796 (7th Cir. 1999).
14. *Id.* at 802.
15. Koenick v. Felton, 190 F. 3d 259 (4th Cir. 1999).
16. *Id.* at 267.

… April—Good Friday

APRIL FOOLS!

On April 1, 2013, popular law site JDSupra.com fooled some readers in the legal community when it published the following article:[1]

In a closely watched case, Ayeprel v. Phules, the Supreme Judicial Court of Massachusetts formally recognized that confidential communications between so-called "work spouses" may be privileged. The 5–4 decision makes Massachusetts the first state in the country to adopt such a privilege.

The genesis of this ruling dates back to 2008, when Marcus Ayeprel was accused through an anonymous posting on his company's intranet site of having embezzled funds from the company's March Madness office pool. Believing that his colleague, Judith Phules, was behind the allegations of embezzlement, Ayeprel sued Phules for defamation and intentional infliction of emotional distress. Because Ayeprel knew that Phules had a particularly close relationship with another coworker, Sidney Finch, Ayeprel sought to depose Finch to uncover whether Phules had admitted to him her involvement in the intranet posting. While Finch admitted generally that he and Phules had discussed what appeared to be discrepancies in the March Madness pool proceeds, Finch refused to divulge the substance of his conversations with Phules. When pressed to justify his objection, Finch's counsel said that the conversations were privileged because Finch and Phules were "work spouses who intended such communications to remain in confidence."

Ayeprel moved to compel disclosure of the Phules-Finch conversations, and the Superior Court ordered Finch to reveal them at a second deposition. Before that deposition took place, however,

---

1. http://www.jdsupra.com/legalnews/work-spouse-privilege-recognized-by-ma-06249/.

The Little Book of Holiday Law

Phules appealed, and the Supreme Judicial Court took the issue for its own direct appellate review. The SJC then reversed the ruling of the Superior Court based on the following reasoning:

> Many employees share confidential information related to their jobs and/or work environment with a work-place confidant whom they trust never to repeat what is communicated between the two. Today, we not only acknowledge that such "work spouse" relationships exist, but we also hold that confidential communications between work spouses are privileged from disclosure unless both agree to waive that privilege.

As the case ultimately makes clear, the work spouse privilege applies only to *verbal* communications:

1. Between two co-workers who have a purely *platonic relationship*;
2. Where the subject matter of the communication is *work-related*; and
3. If the co-workers who are parties to the communication have a history of exchanging confidential information about their jobs, their employer or working environment for a period of at least *6 months*.

While *Ayeprel* involved work spouses of the opposite sex, the decision does not hinge on this fact, and experts agree that same-sex work spouses could invoke the new privilege as well.

So what can or should in-house counsel do in light of the formal recognition of the work spouse privilege? Some have suggested that companies should ask employees to formally declare who, if anyone, is their work spouse so that employers at least can know which communications might be privileged and avoid any risk of what has become known as "work spouse polygamy." Others, such as civil rights advocates in my office, insist that any such mandate would violate the Massachusetts Constitution.

This much is for sure: work spouses are here to stay—at least, that is, until they get work divorces. . . .

Chapter Five

May
A History of Law Day

The first Law Day was established in 1958 by President Eisenhower, in an effort to mark the nation's commitment to the rule of law. Congress designated May 1 as the official date for celebrating Law Day in 1961. Since then, every president has issued a proclamation on May 1 to celebrate Law Day and the rule of law.[1]

One author describes the history of Law Day as follows:

> May Day can be traced to a Welshman who managed a cotton mill in Manchester, England. He envisioned an arrangement by which labor and management would share the rewards of his factory and he chose the First of May, 1833, to celebrate his vision. Soviets picked up the concept and distributed May Day leaflets in St. Petersburg on May 1, 1914. A million Russian workers participated in the May Day strikes. After the 1917 Revolution, Russian

---

1. http://www.americanbar.org/groups/public_education/initiatives_awards/law_day_2013/history_and_archives.html.

Communists declared May Day a great holiday, exhorting workers of the world to unite and throw off the shackles that bound them. In the 1920s, Moscow's Red Square became the scene of massive military reviews of armed power. In this country, the American Communist Party began holding May Day rallies in the mid-1920s, and in 1935, it is said, thirty thousand American Communists demonstrated in New York City. In 1947, the United States Veterans of Foreign Wars designated May 1st as "Loyalty Day," a day to "reaffirm loyalty to the United States of America" to counter the American Communist Party's May Day celebration, and urged Americans to "fly the U.S. flag and observe Loyalty Day in schools and other suitable places with appropriate ceremonies." The next year, Loyalty Day was celebrated by a parade in New York City attended by an estimated 750,000 people in response to the American Communist Party march.

Charles Rhyne, profoundly disturbed by the communist May Day celebrations, began a crusade to establish Law Day, "a day to celebrate the equality and human rights under law and try to convey that message to those enslaved behind the Iron Curtain." Rhyne enlisted the help of Senators John Foster Dulles and Prescott Bush (father of President George H.W. Bush) and together they decided that a Presidential Proclamation would be the best way to establish Law Day. Rhyne, president of the American Bar Association in 1957, took his proposed Proclamation to the then Secretary of State John Foster Dulles, who sent it to the White House for the President's signature.[2]

---

2. Charles A. Saunders, *The Origins of Law Day*, 36 Hous. L. Rev. 42 (June 1999).

May—A History of Law Day

The actual statute proclaiming May 1 as Law Day follows:

a. **Designation.**— May 1 is Law Day, U.S.A.
b. **Purpose.**— Law Day, U.S.A., is a special day of celebration by the people of the United States—
   1. in appreciation of their liberties and the reaffirmation of their loyalty to the United States and of their rededication to the ideals of equality and justice under law in their relations with each other and with other countries; and
   2. for the cultivation of the respect for law that is so vital to the democratic way of life.
c. **Proclamation.**— The President is requested to issue a proclamation—
   1. calling on all public officials to display the flag of the United States on all Government buildings on Law Day, U.S.A.; and
   2. inviting the people of the United States to observe Law Day, U.S.A., with appropriate ceremonies and in other appropriate ways, through public entities and private organizations and in schools and other suitable places.[3]

Law Day, of course, celebrates the rule of law. As one author explains:

> The Rule of Law is the principle that the government must exercise power only in accordance with lawfully enacted and fully disclosed laws that apply equally to all citizens,

---

3. 36 U.S.C. § 113.

regardless of rank, prestige or power. The Rule of Law defends against the arbitrary enforcement of laws characteristic of totalitarian governments like that from which the Founders declared our nation's independence.

The Rule of Law makes our way of life possible. Our form of government and our system of laws are all predicated on the belief that the Rule of Law supersedes all personal ambition or power. The Rule of Law requires that even the government itself is subservient to its own laws. Our nation's adherence to the Rule of Law has created an atmosphere of security, equality and opportunity that has allowed freedom, both personal and economic, to blossom and thrive. The Rule of Law has gone far to conquer injustice and level playing fields in all aspects of life, making this concept truly fundamental.

Unfortunately, the Rule of Law is often taken for granted. Seldom do we stop to recognize that the Rule of Law provides the foundation for our free and democratic society. In 1958, President Dwight D. Eisenhower offered Americans and the world a reminder.[4]

---

4. J. Cliff McKinney & Gwendolyn L. Rucker, *Law Day: Fifty Years of Celebrating the Rule of Law*, 43 Ark. Law. 42 (2008).

May—A History of Law Day

> ### Holiday Fast Facts—May and June
>
> Though barbeque is widely associated with Dad, National Barbeque Month actually takes place in May, the same month as Mother's Day. May also recognizes National Smile Month, National Meditation Month (clearly, something most Moms can use), and, disturbingly, International Audit Month.
>
> June, during which Father's Day is celebrated, also happens to be International Men's Month, National Camping Month, and, perhaps Dad's favorite—National Bathroom Reading Month.[1]
>
> ---
>
> 1. *See* http://www.brownielocks.com/.

Of course, not everyone was happy about a nationally recognized holiday that, as some believed, was in place to recognize the lawyers. One author explains:

> The world was a different place when the first Law Day was held. Rhyne, a 45-year-old Washington, D.C., lawyer who was legal counsel to President Eisenhower for a time, was serving in 1957–58 as the ABA's youngest president to date. His relationship with the administration made it easier to get Eisenhower to issue a proclamation declaring May 1, 1958, as a day to commemorate the rule of law and freedom in the United States.
>
> In a speech in 2000 at the Law Library of Congress, Rhyne explained why he had proposed the creation of Law Day.
>
> "The immediate inspiration for a May 1 celebration of law was directly related to the Cold War," said Rhyne, who died

in 2003. "For many years, the American news media gave front-page headlines and pictures to the Soviet Union's May Day parade of new war weapons. My idea was to contrast the United States' reliance on the rule of law with the Soviet Union's rule by force."

Rhyne's idea struck a chord. Time magazine even marked the first Law Day by featuring him on the cover of its issue for May 5, 1958.

But Rhyne recalled in his 2000 speech that Law Day almost was torpedoed by a misunderstanding among some of Eisenhower's advisers.

While he was in the Oval Office going over the draft proclamation with Eisenhower, said Rhyne, White House Chief of Staff Sherman Adams "burst in yelling, 'Do not sign that paper praising lawyers!'"

But Eisenhower "held up his hand for silence until he had read the entire document," said Rhyne. "Then he said, 'Sherm, this proclamation does not contain one word praising lawyers. It praises our constitutional system of government, our great heritage under the rule of law, and asks our people to stand up and praise what they have created. I like it, and I am going to sign it.'"[5]

Today's Law Day entails community service, teaching about the law, and attorneys working together to discuss and disseminate the importance of the rule of law to a wide audience. Cold War themes aside, more than 50 years later, much is to be learned from the first Law Day celebration. As a past president of the American Bar Association wrote:

---

5. Jason Krause, *Charlie Rhyne's Big Idea: After 50 Years, Law Day Is Still Vital to Building Support for Justice Principles*, 94 A.B.A. J. 65 (2008).

May—A History of Law Day

In a radio address delivered on the first Law Day, ABA past-president Charles S. Rhyne described the day as an opportunity to express "our admiration and respect for the rule of law."

Rhyne called Law Day a time "to recognize the tremendous contribution the law has made in our way of life as a promoter of our progress and as an insurer of the human rights which made that progress possible."

Rhyne recognized in that radio address that Law Day and the rule of law are essential to a broad cross section of our communities, not just lawyers:

"It is law that brings order into the affairs of men, that enables them to lift their sights above mere survival, to accumulate possessions, to develop the arts, to pursue knowledge and to enjoy life among their fellows. Law gives the individual security that he could obtain in no other way; it protects the family and other groups organized for advancement of common interests; it permits the growth of great cities and the development of vast enterprises. In other words, it is the cement that holds our free society together."[6]

---

6. William H. Neukom, *Strengthening Our Foundation: 50th Law Day Will Be a Multidisciplinary Celebration of the Rule of Law in Our Society*, 94 A.B.A. J. 9 (2008).

The Little Book of Holiday Law

HAPPY BELATED LAW DAY!

What This Holiday Needs Is Some Good Cheer (and Presents)

Sean Carter[1]

Three weeks ago, the dreams started again.

Actually, they are more like nightmares, and they all follow the same pattern. I'm late for a very important speech, but for the life of me, I can't find my pants. No matter where I look for them—my closet, the hamper or even the refrigerator (hey, you don't know my housekeeper)—I can't find them. Finally, I decide to leave for the speech anyway, hoping that no one will notice as long as I stay hidden behind the lectern.

Of course, in my dream I never quite take into account that in order to get to the podium, I have to walk through a banquet room of 200 to 300 people, one of whom *might* notice that I'm not exactly wearing "formal attire." Yet, the die is already cast (i.e., I've already spent the deposit for my services). Therefore, I attempt to walk into the banquet room as if nothing is wrong.

I never get more than a few steps before the giggles begin. Eventually, they turn into a cacophony of laughter, which fortunately wakes me from my nightmare.

Over the years, I've had several variations of this dream, and during this time, I've learned the dream's purpose. It is my subconscious mind's way of telling me that I'm woefully unprepared for an important event in my life and that I need to get on the ball or else be caught with my pants down. Well, it's either that or I need a new housekeeper.

---

1. Sean Carter, *Happy Belated Law Day! What This Holiday Needs Is Some Good Cheer (and Presents)*, 4 A.B.A. J. (2005).

May—A History of Law Day

Going with the former conclusion, I've racked my brain for the last three weeks to discover what I was forgetting. Well, today, I discovered the answer, but sadly, too late.

I forgot to observe . . . you guessed it . . . *Law Day*.

I can't believe it! Over the last three years, I have dedicated my life to educating the public about the laws that affect them on a daily basis (so long as it does not require me to wake up before noon). How could I, of all people, forget the most legally sacrosanct day of the year? As I see it, this is like the pope forgetting Easter or the president forgetting the Fourth of July or one of my clients forgetting to bring the balance of my fee to the speech. In other words, it's inexcusable!

Even worse, in more than a decade of being a lawyer, I've somehow managed to forget to observe Law Day every single year. And I don't suspect that I'm alone here. Very few lawyers give any thought to Law Day, at least not the ones I know. Perhaps this explains why I've never received a call on May 1 from a colleague singing, "Happy Law Day to you! Happy Law Day to you!"

This is sad. How is this holiday ever supposed to catch on if most lawyers don't even observe it?

Of course, here lies part of the problem. How do we properly observe Law Day? Do we run through the streets like Old Testament prophets yelling, "Keep the law! Keep the law! Blackstone 3:16"? Or do we take a more subtle approach by burning incense in our homes and preparing burnt offerings? (On second thought, considering that this latter ceremony closely approximates dinner at my home on most evenings, perhaps I've been celebrating Law Day all along and didn't know it.)

In any event, I'm becoming convinced that we need to find a fun and exciting way to celebrate this holiday. That way, lawyers and laypeople alike will actually look forward to Law Day.

The Little Book of Holiday Law

Perhaps one solution is to incorporate lots of drinking into the festivities. You don't see people forgetting to celebrate Cinco de Mayo or St. Patrick's Day, do you? I know I never do. To tell the truth, I'd celebrate Genghis Khan Day if the bars served two-for-one drink specials.

Another possible solution is to start the tradition of exchanging Law Day gifts. This would not only be good for the legal profession but the overall economy as well. We could even go so far as to create our own lovable Law Day hero Santa Clarence. Every May 1, Santa Clarence could come down from the U.S. Supreme Court in a sled pulled by eight Supreme Court interns and hand out writs of habeas corpus to all the children who have been nice throughout the year. (OK, I admit this idea needs work, but you get the point.)

In fact, if we really want to go all out, we could create an entire season devoted to the holiday. Can you just imagine a second season each year of peace on Earth and goodwill toward men? I can see it now. People meeting one another on the streets saying, "Legal Greetings!" Children caroling through the neighborhood, singing classics like "'Twas the Night Before Oral Argument" and "I Saw Mommy Suing Santa Claus."

It gets me all misty-eyed just thinking about it.

And remember, my friends, it's never too early to start preparing for Law Day . . . What better way to say "Happy Law Day" to that special person in your life than buying him or her a copy of my book, *If It Does Not Fit, Must You Acquit*? And if you need a Santa Clarence to appear at your law firm or bar organization event, give me a call. I promise to wear pants.

Chapter Six

June
Holidays and Labor Law: Paid and Unpaid Holidays under Federal and State Labor Laws

Clearly, employers may not discriminate against their employees on the basis of their religious beliefs. But just what "religious beliefs" are protected under the law? Should a court have to decide what beliefs are, indeed, "religious enough" in the protection of employees' beliefs?

The Massachusetts Supreme Judicial Court took a hard look at this issue in 1996, in the case of *Pielech v. Massasoit Greyhound, Inc.*, which involved a Massachusetts statute.[1] That statute had prohibited employers from requiring their employees to violate or forgo any practice of their "creed or religion as required by that creed or religion."[2] The case was filed by two devout Roman Catholic employees of the Raynham-Taunton Greyhound Track, who claimed they were required to work on December 25; when they did not show up to work even though their requests for time off were denied, they suffered adverse actions by their employer. The two women

---

1. Pielech v. Massasoit Greyhound, Inc., 668 N.E. 2d 1298 (Mass. 1996).
2. *See* Mass. Gen. Laws ch. 151B, § 4(1A).

claimed that their employer illegally imposed terms and conditions on them, compliance with which would require them to forgo the practices and requirements of their religious beliefs.[3]

The court invalidated the Massachusetts statute in question, holding that it violated the Establishment Clause on two grounds: first, it privileged organized religions over others, and second, it required courts to resolve disputes regarding religious dogma, which resulted in excessive entanglement of church and state.[4]

Another case involved a plaintiff employee of the Commonwealth of Puerto Rico, who sued the territory after she alleged she had been discriminated against. The plaintiff, a devout Pentecostal Christian, objected to the decoration of government offices with witches and goblins during the Halloween season, claiming that the decorations amounted to a celebration of paganism, which was offensive to her religious beliefs.[5] The employee also claimed that she was retaliated against and suffered a hostile work environment.

The district court concluded that the employee did not state a claim for religious discrimination.

> The government conduct that plaintiff challenges as offensive to the Establishment Clause is the display of traditional Halloween decorations in her office. There is no allegation in her amended complaint beyond that of a mere display of decorations in the overall setting of the celebration of Halloween festivities. The cats, goblins or screeching mat alone do not convey an endorsement of any religious belief. Such decorations, like Halloween costumes and parties, are linked to the seasonal celebration of a fun-loving tradition in which

---

3. *Pielech*, 668 N.E. 2d at 1300.
4. *Id.* at 1303.
5. Rosa-Ruiz v. Gonzalez-Galoffin, 2007 WL 2768694 (D. Puerto Rico 2007).

June—Holidays and Labor Law

children are particularly involved in classrooms, neighborhood gatherings and trick or treating. Halloween decorations, like valentines, Easter bunnies, and egg hunts are all secular displays and activities that neither convey religious messages nor constitute religious symbols. Halloween lost its religious and superstitious overtones long ago. It has become instead a commercial holiday enjoyed by communities in its many forms of entertainment.[6]

In another case, an Orthodox Jewish employee sued his employer, a national telecommunications company, claiming religious discrimination.[7] The employee claimed that one of his supervisors "stormed off" during his job interview when he informed the supervisor that he would need time off for Jewish holidays and had to leave work early enough on Fridays to be home for the Shabbat. After three weeks on the job, the employee sent his manager a five-page handwritten letter detailing numerous complaints, including complaints about having to share work tools and not having his own workstation. Over the next few weeks, he reminded his supervisor about needing time off for Jewish holidays, and claimed the supervisor expressed reluctance to grant it, then retaliated against him by moving him to the night shift.

Eventually, the employee filed a complaint with the Equal Employment Opportunity Commission (EEOC), but the EEOC declined to pursue his claims. He then sued the company in federal court, and the court granted judgment without a trial to the employer. The U.S. Court of Appeals affirmed, holding that the employee did not prove he was discriminated against on the basis of his religion. He was not treated any differently than other employees, the court noted, and he didn't prove that the reason the employer gave for moving

---

6. *Id.* at 4.
7. Freedman v. MCI Telecommunications Corp., No. 00-7238 (D.C. Cir. 2001).

him to the night shift (which was to provide him with better training) was a cover story for religious discrimination.[8]

And what about provisions for holiday time? There is, actually, no federal law that mandates an employer to provide for time off during holidays. Employers are not required to pay hourly employees for time off during holidays, and are required, generally, only to pay employees for time actually worked—salaried employees, who are given a holiday off, however, must be paid their full weekly salaries if working any hours during the week of the holiday. Explains one author:[9]

> You may attach conditions to holiday pay if it is part of the employee's employment contract or it is otherwise in writing. You do not have to provide the same holiday benefits to all employees as long as the different treatment is not discriminatory. For instance, you can provide holiday pay to full-time employees but not part-time employees. Although it is common to pay a premium to employees who work certain holidays, you are not legally required to do so. The decision to pay an increased wage for holiday work is made at the employer's discretion as an incentive for employees to work the holiday.[10]

The issue of paid holidays is treated differently across the globe. In Kuwait, for example, "an employee is entitled to one full day off per week with pay. The traditional day off is Friday, but this may be adjusted according to the requirements of the work. An employee also has the right to 13 public holidays each year with full pay."[11]

---

8. *Id.*
9. Hillary Collyer, *Accommodating Employees' Religious Practices During the Holidays*, *in* 19 VIRGINIA EMPLOYMENT LAW LETTER 4 (2007).
10. *Id.*
11. Business Laws of Kuwait § 5:7 (database updated on Westlaw Feb. 2013).

June—Holidays and Labor Law

Likewise, in Saudi Arabia,

Friday is the day of rest. Thus the "weekend" in Saudi Arabia is, in effect, one day, though many companies work on Thursdays for only half of the day.[12] . . . There are two recognized holidays in the Kingdom which are in accordance with the Kingdom's Basic Law. These holidays are Eid Al-Fitr and Eid Al-Adha. Subsequently, the Government added September 23, which is the Saudi national day. It is usual for government offices to close for up to a week during both Eid holidays, which are considered moveable feasts. Private sector offices are usually closed for a shorter period of time.[13]

Clearly, if an American employer provides for time off during holidays, it cannot discriminate against employees based on their particular beliefs and ensuing celebrations. Note:

Under Title VII, an employer's holiday leave policies and practices must not favor one religion over another. Thus, a Protestant employee's allegations that the employer granted paid religious holidays to members of certain religions, which resulted in their receiving more paid holidays than he did and in his having to work more overtime and accepting undesirable assignments, stated a claim of religious discrimination under Title VII. . . .[14] Title VII requires that holiday leave policies and practices treat all religions equally. Such policies need not be drawn either so broadly or narrowly as to suit

---

12. Business Laws of Saudi Arabia § 8:14 (database updated on Westlaw Aug. 2012).
13. Id.
14. 1 Emp. Discrim. Coord. Analysis of Federal Law § 33:2, citing to Ka Nam Kuan v. City of Chicago, 563 F. Supp. 255, 32 Fair Empl. Prac. Cas. (BNA) 566, 33 Empl. Prac. Dec. (CCH) P34093 (N.D. Ill. 1983).

every employee's religious needs, but must provide a reasonable accommodation to the religious needs of employees who request such accommodations (Fed L §§ 1:1 et seq.).[15]

Several states have specific laws in place regarding this issue. For example, a Texas law states that

> An institution of higher education may not discriminate against or penalize a faculty member who is absent from work for the observance of a religious holy day and who gives proper notice of that absence, if the customary and generally applicable practices of the institution permit general personal absence by faculty members.[16]

In fact, at least one state has imposed criminal penalties for failing to reimburse employees or pay vacation, separation, or holiday benefits (although the law may be preempted by federal laws):

> An employer who fails to pay the amounts agreed for the reimbursement of expenses to employees or for vacation, separation, or holiday pay within the required time is guilty of a misdemeanor punishable by a fine of $500 to $20,000, imprisonment for no more than one year, or both. If the employer is a corporation, the corporation's president, secretary, treasurer, or other officers exercising corresponding functions may be affected by those punishments.[17]

---

15. *Id.*
16. *See* 12 Tex. Jur. 3d *Colleges and Universities* § 42 (database updated on Westlaw Jul. 2012).
17. N.Y. Lab. Law § 198-c(1) (2008).

June—Holidays and Labor Law

A frequent issue that comes up in the workplace deals with holiday decorations. As one article put it: "Religious practices and diversity are increasing in the United States, and that trend is presenting new challenges for employers. One common form of religious expression that affects the workplace involves employees' requests for accommodations to observe their religious holidays."[18]

Under Title VII of the U.S. Code, employers are prohibited from discriminating against employees on the basis of religion, which includes all aspects of religious observance and practice as well as religious beliefs. Employers "must accommodate a current or prospective employee's religious observance or practice unless doing so would cause . . . an undue hardship."[19]

The article notes that both "reasonable accommodation" and "undue hardship" must be viewed case by case, and offers the following suggestions:[20]

You may be able to offer reasonable accommodations by:

- providing flexible scheduling;
- allowing voluntary substitution of assignments;
- offering unpaid leave to observe a religious holiday (unless you offer paid leave for all other time off, in which case you must give paid leave);
- offering staggered work hours; or
- allowing employees to make up hours by working longer shifts.

---

18. *Finding Holiday Harmony with a Diverse Workforce, in* 15 Wyoming Employment Law Letter 2 (Bradley T. Cave & Joanna R. Vilos eds., 2010).
19. *Id.*
20. *Id.*

An undue hardship occurs when an accommodation would impose more than a small cost or cause more than a minor disruption to your operations. Here are some questions to help determine whether an accommodation will present an undue hardship:

- What will it cost? You don't have to go to great expense, and religious accommodation requirements are less extensive than those for disabled employees.
- What will it mean to your business? If the accommodation will disrupt the business, it's more likely to pose an undue hardship.
- Will it violate a collective bargaining agreement or breach a contract? If so, no accommodation is required.
- Will it infringe on others' religious rights? A "yes" answer indicates undue hardship.
- Will it cause safety problems? Again, a "yes" indicates undue hardship.

If you choose not to accommodate an employee, make sure you have documentation to support your decision.

In some cases, the courts have held that a private employer could not be held to accommodate an employee's observance of the Sabbath where it constituted an undue hardship, such as substantial incurrence of costs or difficulty maintaining seniority rights.[21]

---

21. *See, e.g.,* U.S.-Gibson v. Missouri Pacific R.R., 620 F. Supp. 85 (E.D. Ark. 1985), and U.S.-Johnson v. U.S. Postal Service, 364 F. Supp. 37 (N.D. Fla. 1973).

Chapter Seven

July
Holidays and Court Procedures

Generally speaking, common law has held that judicial proceedings cannot be held nor judicial acts performed on Sunday. Explains one annotation,[1]

> While in the absence of statute a ministerial act in connection with judicial proceedings, and, according to many cases, quasi-judicial acts, such as the issuance and service of process, performed on Sundays are valid, in jurisdictions where the common law prevails, the right or authority to perform any judicial act on Sunday must be derived from a statute conferring that right or authority, and a statute conferring such right should, like any other statute in derogation of common law, be strictly construed. There are various limitations upon and exceptions to the rule forbidding the performance of judicial acts on Sunday, based largely upon convenience

---

1. R.P. Davis, *Validity of Court's Judgment Rendered on Sunday or Holiday*, 85 A.L.R. 2d 595 (2007).

and necessity, such, for example, as the right to receive the verdict of a jury on Sunday. And it is generally recognized that when a case has been submitted to the jury before Sunday, the court may give on Sunday additional instructions to the jury then deliberating upon it. A jury may also be discharged on Sunday. A court may validly enter an order of adjournment if it has authority to sit for any purpose on that day. The courts do not regard statutory or legal holidays as nonjuridical days unless constrained to do so by the terms or the necessary effect of statutes. A legal holiday has only the sanctity attached to it by statute. It is a dies non juridicus only when expressly made so by statute, and even then only to the extent specified in the act. Statutory holidays do not have the sacredness of the Sabbath, and any legal business may be transacted and any legal act performed upon a holiday other than that which is positively or by necessary implication forbidden by the terms of a statutory enactment. Hence, it is generally held that courts may sit and try causes on legal holidays, unless the statutes, by force of their terms or necessary effect, prohibit them from doing so. This construction has been given to statutes, so as to permit judicial proceedings on January 1, Washington's Birthday, Good Friday, the Fourth of July, Labor Day, Thanksgiving Day, and Saturday half holidays. Similarly, unless a statute expressly forbids, an indictment may be found and returned on a holiday.

The validity of service of process on Sundays and holidays has been the subject of a few cases. (Some states, such as New York, expressly prohibit service or execution of all legal process on Sundays, except where otherwise authorized by law.[2] In fact, New York

---

2. *See* 3B CARMODY-WAIT 2D, CYCLOPEDIA OF NEW YORK PRACTICE WITH FORMS

July—Holidays and Court Procedures

also provides that service on the Sabbath or a religious holiday with the knowledge that the person being served observes that holiday constitutes malice.[3])

In some cases, the courts have held Sunday service as valid—even though judicial proceedings could not properly be performed on a Sunday, the service of process constituted merely a ministerial act that was not prohibited. Some examples include an Alabama domestic relations case[4] and a Mississippi case stemming from the shooting of a dog.[5] Other courts have held Sunday service to be invalid, most of them relying on specific state statutes such as the New York one mentioned above.[6]

Of course, holidays can also greatly affect deadlines in court. In federal courts, the following rules apply:

> For purpose of computation of time, when the period is stated in days or a longer unit of time, include the last day of the period, but if the last day is a Saturday, Sunday, or legal holiday, the period continues to run until the end of the next day that is not a Saturday, Sunday, or legal holiday. Unless a different time is set by a statute, local rule, or court order, the last day ends, for electronic filing, at midnight in the court's time zone; and for filing by other means, the last day ends when the clerk's office is scheduled to close.
>
> The next day is determined by continuing to count forward when the period is measured after an event and backward when measured before an event. When the period is stated in

---

§ 24:87 (database updated on Westlaw Sept. 2013).
   3. *See* 3A Carmody-Wait 2d, Cyclopedia of New York Practice with Forms § 24:30 (database updated on Westlaw Sept. 2013).
   4. *See* Calhoun v. Calhoun, 46 Ala. App. 381 (1970).
   5. *See* Robb v. Ward, 266 So. 2d 133 (Miss. 1972).
   6. *See, e.g.*, Hessel v. Hessel, 164 N.Y.S. 2d 519 (1957); Cutler v. Cutler, 217 N.Y.S. 2d 185 (1961); and Mintz v. Frink, 217 N.C. 101 (1940).

hours, if the period would end on a Saturday, Sunday, or legal holiday, the period continues to run until the same time on the next day that is not a Saturday, Sunday, or legal holiday.[7]

In one case, the Missouri Court of Appeals held that, in fact, a holiday is not a holiday unless the legislature says it is. The case involved a motion for a new trial that was filed the Monday after the Thanksgiving holiday in 1996 by the defendant in a civil case. The issue? The defendant had 90 days to file the motion—if the Friday after Thanksgiving was a legal holiday, then the motion was timely on the day filed; however, if it was deemed not to be so, then the motion should have been filed the Friday prior.[8]

> ### Holiday Fast Facts—Adams, Jefferson, and Monroe
>
> Two famous lawyers and presidents both died on the Fourth of July in 1826: John Adams and Thomas Jefferson. Exactly five years later, in 1831, James Monroe also died on July fourth.

The court rejected the defendant's argument that two memoranda that permitted courts to be closed for business the Friday after Thanksgiving had the effect of making the day a legal holiday. In fact, the court said, the definition of legal holiday was confined to those days that were specifically designated as holidays by state statute.

Another case in California, however, held that the Friday after Thanksgiving was, in fact, a legal holiday for purposes of

---

7. 4 CYCLOPEDIA OF FEDERAL PROCEDURE § 13:4 (3d ed., 2013).
8. Heinen v. Healthline Management, Inc., 982 S.W.2d 244 (Mo. banc 1998).

July—Holidays and Court Procedures

the bankruptcy rule governing computation of time. In that case, the former spouse of a Chapter 7 debtor filed an adversary proceeding to except debt from discharge, and the debtor moved to dismiss, claiming that the proceeding was untimely when filed on the Monday following Thanksgiving. The court of appeals held for the claimant and reversed on the dismissal. The court noted that court personnel treated the Friday after Thanksgiving as a judicial holiday—for example, documents presented to the clerks on that Friday were not filed until the following Monday—thereby making it a legal holiday for practitioners.

Of course, when it comes to computing time periods, "days are days," at least under the 2009 changes to the Federal Rules of Civil Procedure. Intervening holidays, in other words, do not extend the time period on which something becomes due. The Amendments were adopted in part to clarify the rules regarding time computation.[9]

The bottom line for clients and practitioners alike? Always check your local court rules on holidays before filing!

---

9. *See* Traci T. McKnee, *Saturdays, Sundays and Holidays Count: The 2009 Amendments to the Federal Rules of Civil Procedure*, 29 TRIAL ADVOC. Q. 16 (2010).

Holiday Fast Facts—The Fourth of July

The first official Fourth of July celebration occurred in Philadelphia in 1777, one year after the colonies voted for and officially declared independence.[1] The celebration included fireworks, music, bonfires, bells ringing, and gunshots being fired. Bunting, or decorated pieces of cloth, was displayed.

During America's centennial celebration in 1876, the centennial Exposition—a lot like the world's fair—was held, and during it Alexander Graham Bell introduced the telephone.[2] In 1976, when America celebrated its 200th birthday, the bicentennial party on the Fourth of July featured 212 sailing ships in New York Harbor, sailing from more than 30 nations.[3] On July 4, 1960, the first American flag to bear all 50 stars was raised.[4]

The Fourth of July, of course, stands for freedom, patriotism, and the birth of the union. The word "patriotism" stems from the Latin word "patria," meaning "homeland" or "fatherland."[5]

The first image of Uncle Sam was introduced on a World War I recruitment poster, bearing the slogan "I Want You." It became adopted as a national symbol in 1961.[6]

---

1. CASS R. SANDAK, PATRIOTIC HOLIDAYS 11 (1990).
2. *Id.* at 12.
3. *Id.*
4. *Id.* at 42.
5. *Id.* at 12.
6. JIM MCCANN & JEANNE BENEDICT, CELEBRATIONS: A JOYOUS GUIDE TO HOLIDAYS FROM PAST TO PRESENT 83–84 (2001).

Chapter Eight

August

Holidays and Business Law: The Effect of Holidays on Business Filings and Acts

In business, a deadline is a deadline, right? Sure, but there may be an exception if that deadline falls on a legal holiday. "As a general rule, when the last day for the performance of an act falls on a legal holiday on which the act cannot legally be done, the period will be extended and the act may be done on the following business day," notes one encyclopedia entry.[1] The entry also notes that the rule does not typically apply to "extend the time for an act which must be performed 'not less than' or 'not later than' a given number of days before a designated time," along with some other exceptions, such as when the day is designated a legal holiday only for limited purposes and the act in question is not included among them.[2]

Certain government filings are, therefore, extended due to holidays. As an example:

---

1. 86 C.J.S. Time § 40 (database updated on Westlaw Sept. 2013).
2. *Id.*

The Little Book of Holiday Law

Generally, the Internal Revenue Code provides that when the due date for filing a form or document falls on a Saturday, Sunday, or day that is a legal holiday in the District of Columbia, the filing is timely if made on the next succeeding business day—that is, a day that is not a Saturday, Sunday, or legal holiday.[3]

In fact, some states also provide for extensions of time if the performance of an act falls on a weekend or holiday. In Ohio, for example,

[t]he time within which an act is required by law to be done is computed by excluding the first and including the last day, except when the last day falls on a Sunday or a legal holiday, then the act may be done on the next succeeding day which is not a Sunday or a legal holiday. This statute has been interpreted to extend the time for payment of rent in accordance with the general rule.[4]

Likewise, in New Jersey, "[i]f the day fixed for the termination of a lease falls on Sunday or on a legal holiday, the tenant may, without legal liability, vacate the premises on the next business day."[5]

As for negotiable instruments, according to one annotation,[6]

---

3. Sydney S. Traum & Judith Rood Traum, The S Corporation Answer Book TSCAB Q 2:7 (2013).
4. 65 Ohio Jur. 3d *Landlord and Tenant* § 279 (database updated on Westlaw Sept. 2013).
5. Raymond I. Korona, *Landlord and Tenant Law, in* 23A New Jersey Practice Series § 40.112 (5th ed.) (database updated on Westlaw Jun. 2013).
6. 102 A.L.R. 437 (1936). ("Construction, application, and effect of provision of Uniform Negotiable Instruments Law, or other statute, relating to maturity or time for presentment of negotiable paper which falls due on Saturday, Sunday, or holiday.")

August—Holidays and Business Law

[i]n the absence of statute, it is settled, as a part of the law merchant, that when a note or bill is payable with grace, and the third day of grace falls on Sunday, or any other holiday on which money is not usually paid, it becomes due on the second day of grace, namely, on Saturday. The days of grace being an indulgence, it is deemed to be perfectly consistent to require payment on the second day of grace to avoid giving four days of grace. But when there are no days of grace, and the time for payment or performance specified in the contract falls on Sunday, the debtor may discharge his obligation on the following day. The Uniform Negotiable Instruments Law provides: "Every negotiable instrument is payable at the time fixed therein without grace. When the day of maturity falls upon Sunday, or a holiday, the instrument is payable on the next succeeding business day. Instruments falling due or becoming payable on Saturday are to be presented for payment on the next succeeding business day, except that instruments payable on demand may, at the option of the holder, be presented for payment before 12 o'clock noon on Saturday when that entire day is not a holiday."[7]

7. *Id.*

Chapter Nine

September
Official State and Local Holidays, from Secular to Religious

What makes a holiday a "legal holiday?" Federal, state, and local governments alike can designate days on which official business is closed and citizens enjoy time off.

The *Cyclopedia of Federal Procedure* defines a legal holiday as follows:

A. the day set aside by statute for observing New Year's Day, Martin Luther King Jr.'s Birthday, Washington's Birthday, Memorial Day, Independence Day, Labor Day, Columbus Day, Veterans' Day, Thanksgiving Day, or Christmas Day;
B. any day declared a holiday by the President or Congress; and
C. for periods that are measured after an event, any other day declared a holiday by the state where the district court is located.[1]

---

1. 4 Cyclopedia of Federal Procedure § 13:5 (3d ed., database updated on Westlaw Aug. 2013).

The Little Book of Holiday Law

Religious holidays may be designated as "legal holidays" by the legislature, so long as they have a secular purpose and do not have the effect of advancing or promoting a particular religion.[2] For some examples, see Chapter Four regarding the constitutionality of the Good Friday holiday. In fact, the government may also recognize the cultural significance of certain holidays, such as Christmas, so long as it does not serve to endorse a particular religion.[3] For some examples, see Chapter One regarding the constitutionality of holiday displays.

> ### Holiday Fast Facts—Constitution Week
>
> In 1956, Congress established Constitution Week, to begin each year on September 17—the date in 1787 when the Constitution was signed by the delegates. In 2005, September 17 was officially designated as Constitution Day and Citizenship Day, requiring schools and public offices to provide educational programs that further a better understanding of the U.S. Constitution.[1]
>
> ---
>
> 1. http://www.senate.gov/artandhistory/history/common/generic/ConstitutionDay.htm.

But the definitions do not simply end with the term "legal holiday." Just look at the following section of California Jurisprudence to see the various definitions involved in designating state holidays:

---

2. *See, e.g.*, Bridenbaugh v. Bannon, 185 F. 3d 796 (7th Cir. 1999).
3. *See, e.g.*, Ganulin v. U.S., 71 F. Supp. 2d 824 (S.D. Ohio 1999), *aff'd*, 238 F. 3d 420 (6th Cir. 2000).

September—Official State and Local Holidays

A holiday is a day that is set apart for worship, to revere the memory of a great leader and benefactor of humanity, to rejoice over some great national or historical event, or to rekindle the flame of an ideal.

The term has also been defined as (1) a consecrated day or religious festival or (2) a day on which the ordinary occupations are suspended, a day of exemption, i.e., cessation from work, a day of festivity, recreation, or amusement.

A "legal holiday" is a day that is validly set apart by statute or executive authority for one or more of the purposes enumerated above but excluding a religious day which, as such, cannot be constitutionally set apart as a public holiday.

The term "legal holiday" appears in certain statutes but is not statutorily defined. For example, the term is used in statutes permitting closure of state offices on legal holidays, permitting a commissioner of marriages to accept fees for performing a marriage on a legal holiday, and permitting closure of the office of the Public Utilities Commission.

It has also been noted that the term "nonjudicial day" is no different from the expression "legal holiday" and simply means a day on which process cannot ordinarily issue or be executed or returned and on which courts do not usually sit.

Observation:

While statutory "judicial holidays" currently include Saturdays, the statute creating the "Saturday half-holiday" in the public offices of the state and political divisions, expressly declares that it does not prevent or invalidate the issuance of any legal process on that half-holiday.

A "special" or "limited" holiday is a holiday applying only to a special class or classes of business, or a special class or classes of persons, and not appointed to be generally observed throughout the state by all classes of business and all classes of persons, while a "general holiday" is one that is not so limited, for example, a day declared a legal holiday by proclamation of the governor, with a request that it be observed by all people generally.

A "general holiday" must be distinguished from a "legal holiday" and "holiday in this state."

Bank holidays are notable examples of special holidays.

The term "personal holiday," as used in the Government Code, refers to the one-day holiday that is granted to and personally selected by every state employee during each calendar year.

Holidays must be distinguished from certain other commemorative days that, though set apart by statute to honor persons, things, or events, are not holidays.[4]

---

4. 37 CAL. JUR. 3D *Holidays* § 1.

Chapter Ten

October
Scary Cases: Halloween Pranks Gone Bad

Halloween pranks and mischief have a long-standing and rich history among American society. As far back as the 19th century, practical jokes and pranks enjoyed a healthy tradition, especially among young men and boys.[1] By the 1920s, however, healthy troublemaking gave way to an increasingly troubling brand of mischief: "Rather than overturn an outhouse or hide a sty fence, revelers were now tempted to steal, set small fires and damage property."[2] To help curb the "Halloween problem," school officials and concerned parents nationwide employed more vigilance in dealing with vandals, whether through increased patrols or stern warnings. By the 1970s, rumors of holiday candy laced with drugs even prompted some towns to outlaw trick-or-treating.[3]

---

    1. Lesley Post Bannatyne, Halloween: An American Holiday, An American History 61 (1998).
    2. *Id.* at 124.
    3. *Id.* at 144–46.

In recent years, Halloween has become quite criminal—and we have the cases to prove it.

In one Georgia case, a defendant became enraged at another man who told him to drive more slowly through a subdivision on Halloween night, as children were trick-or-treating. The defendant began cursing loudly at a group of dads who were imploring him to slow down and watch his language. Being provoked by the defendant to approach his car, one of the dads hit the defendant in the face. After that physical encounter, the defendant pulled a gun, shot the man in the stomach, and pointed the gun at a bystander, an off-duty policeman who tried to intervene. The defendant was subsequently arrested and found guilty of aggravated assault, among a slew of other crimes.[4]

The defendant appealed. One issue on appeal dealt with the Rule of Sequestration regarding witnesses, as the off-duty policeman, who became a witness at trial, was allowed to remain in the courtroom during the proceedings to allow him to assist the prosecutor. The appeals court found no error in permitting the witness to stay. In addition, the defendant argued that the court's instruction to the jury regarding justification was erroneous. The appeals court again disagreed. "[T]he trial court in this case did not charge the jury that an act that is committed in a spirit of revenge is never justifiable," the court noted. "The motive for an act is for the jury to determine, as is the issue of whether a defendant acted under the fears of a reasonable man."[5]

Yet another case, this one in New Hampshire, involved an altercation between a husband and wife. The defendant husband returned home after drinking at work, and continued to drink at home on Halloween night in 2003. His wife handed out candy

---

4. *Jack v. State*, 536 S.E. 2d 235 (Ga. App. 2000).
5. *Id.* at 238.

October—Scary Cases: Halloween Pranks Gone Bad

to trick-or-treaters who came to the door, and all the while the pair bickered back and forth. The defendant made sarcastic comments about the way his wife handed out candy and called her derogatory names. She responded with a derogatory statement of her own and struck her husband, then walked toward her living room to try to get away. The defendant then shoved and hit his wife, causing bruises on her face, leg, and elbow, as well as rug burns.[6]

The defendant was convicted of simple assault. During trial, he asked the court to instruct the jury on self-defense and mutual combat. While the court allowed the instruction on self-defense, it denied the request for a mutual combat instruction. The defendant appealed.

The Supreme Court of New Hampshire affirmed the decision, holding that a mutual combat instruction was inappropriate absent some evidence that the parties agreed to fight. The court noted,

> [The wife] testified that after she slapped the defendant, she went "rapidly" into the living room because she "was trying to get away because [she] was just upset." As she left the room, the defendant hit or pushed her from behind. We conclude that there was no evidence to show an agreement to fight between the defendant and [his wife], either expressly or by implication.[7]

In a case fraught with terror, four men, masquerading as trick-or-treaters with painted faces and costumes, made their way into a victim's home on Halloween in 1997. They ransacked the house looking for money and eventually took $15,000 from the victim's

---

6. State v. Place, 152 N.H. 225 (2005).
7. *Id.* at 228.

safe. They also held the victim and her ten-year-old twin sons at gunpoint, binding their legs, arms, and mouths with duct tape before dumping them in the basement of their home.[8]

The defendants in the case was convicted of home invasion, armed robbery, and kidnapping, among other offenses, and he appealed. A chief issue on appeal dealt with the defendant's fingerprints, which were found on the inside door of a traditional Korean cabinet in the victims' basement. The defendant claimed that the court erred in failing to give a specific jury instruction regarding fingerprint evidence, and that his counsel was ineffective in failing to request one. Specifically, the defendant relied on a footnote in another case stating that "since the defendant might have been in the [the murder victim's] apartment on other occasions, the defendant might have been entitled to a limiting instruction emphasizing that the fingerprints were admitted in evidence to show only that the defendant was present there at some time."[9]

The appeals court disagreed with the defendant and affirmed his conviction. The court noted that not only was there no evidence that the defendant had been inside the victims' home prior to the night of the robbery, but other circumstantial evidence, such as cell phone records, linked the defendant to the scene of the crime on the night in question.

A Texas juvenile was convicted of aggravated robbery after being part of a group that accosted a group of trick-or-treaters. The defendant stood in front of a victim as another perpetrator stood holding a knife to the victim's throat, and demanding the group's candy and Halloween masks. The defendant argued on appeal that the state failed to prove his identity beyond a

---

8. Commonwealth v. Ye, 52 Mass. App. Ct. 390 (2001).
9. *Id.* at 394, citing Commonwealth v. LaCorte, 373 Mass. 700, 702–03 n. 1 (1977).

October—Scary Cases: Halloween Pranks Gone Bad

reasonable doubt, but the appeals court affirmed the juvenile court's conviction.[10]

In a case involving wrongdoing on many levels, a defendant who admitted she was a member of a gang blamed a gang debt she owed on her brother (the two were not biologically related, but referred to each other as siblings). After "serving up" her brother thusly, she acted as a "bridge" between gang members, having sex with several men and facilitating drug sales. The saga ultimately ended on Halloween night with the gang shooting of four young people, two of whom died from gunshot wounds. The shooter, as the court noted, was smiling.[11] "Crank, not the smiling shooter, is the devil in this ghastly Halloween tale," the court noted. "It is hard to imagine the warped world in which the defendant tried to survive, for this is a story of primal survival on the drug dealing, gangbanging, violent streets young addicts populate."[12]

Nine months after the Halloween murders, the defendant was incarcerated for unrelated crimes. In an effort to get out of jail, she initiated contact with the Halloween murder investigators and offered information. Later, the defendant changed her mind. At trial, the defendant's main theory was that her confession—elicited during several interrogations by police—was coerced and false, and therefore should not have been admitted into evidence. The court disagreed, pointing out that her confessions were voluntary, that her narratives were not forthright, and that the police officers' "tough talk" did not become unduly coercive.[13]

In another case, a defendant's habeas corpus petition was denied by a California court, after he was convicted of robbery,

---

10. *In the matter of F.J.S., a juvenile*, 241 S.W.3d 565 (Tex. Ct. App. 2007).
11. People v. Marten, 2007 WL 4296621 (Cal. App. 3d Dist. 2007).
12. *Id.* at 1.
13. *Id.* at 5–7.

burglary, and other offenses, and sentenced to prison for more than 14 years. In that case, the defendant entered the home of an elderly widow on Halloween night (she opened the door to him after he called "trick-or-treat") and pushed her down, taking some earrings and handguns from a dresser drawer.[14]

But criminal law isn't the only area of law implicated in Halloween troublemaking—personal injury is another field involved.

In one case, the plaintiff mother was injured while she was trick-or-treating with her children in a residential subdivision, after she stepped in a hole and fell. She sued the city, claiming it negligently failed to properly maintain a city street or sidewalk, as well as claiming that the hole constituted a nuisance. The hole in question was about three feet long and one and a half feet wide, and it was located in a grassy area about nine feet from the edge of the paved street, within a ten-foot strip that served as a portion of the city's right-of-way.[15]

The court held that the city was not responsible, as there was no evidence that the hole was located in a place where pedestrians ordinarily walked.

> [W]here a plaintiff alleges that the defective condition which caused the injury was located on a part of the city's street and sidewalk system, there must be some evidence that the defect was located in an area accepted by the city, either expressly or by implication, for use as a street or sidewalk, before the city can be charged with liability for negligently failing to maintain the area in a reasonably safe condition.[16]

---

14. Averna v. Sandor, 2012 WL 1413990 (C.D. Cal. 2013).
15. City of Vidalia v. Brown, 237 Ga. App. 831 (1999).
16. *Id.* at 853.

October—Scary Cases: Halloween Pranks Gone Bad

In a sad Ohio case (which thankfully ended well) the plaintiff, a boy, was trick-or-treating with his mother when he darted out to the street between two cars and was hit by the defendant's car. The boy was rushed to the hospital and suffered head and pelvic injuries, but fortunately recovered and returned to a healthy and active life.

The plaintiff and his mother sued the defendant for negligence in the operation of her vehicle. The trial court granted summary judgment for the defendant, and the appeals court affirmed. The court looked carefully at the defendant's conduct and noted that she drove carefully and with a heightened sense of caution, aware that she was driving in a school zone inundated with small children trick-or-treating. In addition, the court noted that the defendant never exceeded the speed limit and drove at all times between 15 and 25 miles per hour, and that the driver attempted to avoid hitting the boy by swerving.[17]

One terrible case speaks of the deadly dangers lurking in the street during Halloween night; the case involved a wrongful death suit against a driver by parents who sought to recover damages for the death and conscious pain and suffering of their young son. The defendant driver filed for summary judgment on the issue of liability, claiming that the victim darted in front of her while crossing the street and was therefore comparatively negligent, but the court denied her motion.[18] The court reasoned: "The accident was located in the vicinity of two schools. It happened on a clear Halloween day. There was nothing obstructing the Defendant's view of the young men and she either never saw or lost sight of the infant-Plaintiff before the accident."[19]

---

17. Kelley v. Shelton, 2001 WL 88846 (Ohio App. 3d Dist. 2001).
18. Wolkis v. Klatch, 34 Misc. 3d 1207(A), 2012 WL 48041 (N.Y. Supp. 2012).
19. *Id.* at 4.

A particular issue in the case dealt with whether the plaintiffs' son experienced pre-accident terror and conscious pain and suffering. The defendants claimed that the victim never regained consciousness and therefore there was no evidence that he suffered any conscious pain, again asking for summary judgment. The court again disagreed, citing to testimony by the parents that the victim was responsive to certain stimuli and conversations while in the hospital; therefore, the court held, the defendants did not establish that he couldn't suffer conscious pain and suffering.[20]

Then there was the case of the grandmother who, on Halloween day, stopped in front of a supermarket to chat with friends, leaving the keys in her car and the motor running. The problem? Her two-year-old grandson was also in the car, unrestrained in a booster seat.[21]

The court describes what happened next:

> It only took a moment for Christine's little nipper to crawl behind the wheel, slip the car into gear, and set it into motion. As the car rolled out of control, it collided with two other cars and two pedestrians. Mrs. O'Neill was the most severely damaged victim of Christine's negligence.
>
> Mrs. O'Neill was in her eighties and could not possibly evade the slow-moving car as it approached her. The insured's vehicle pinned her between it and another car and slowly crushed her trapped body. Mrs. O'Neill was pried loose and airlifted to St. Louis University Trauma Center, where she spent the next month in the intensive care unit. Her body suffered a crushed hip, a broken arm,

---

20. *Id.* at 4–5.
21. O'Neill v. Gallant Ins. Co., 329 Ill. App. 3d 1166 (2002).

October—Scary Cases: Halloween Pranks Gone Bad

four cracked ribs, and two fractured fingers. She lost more than 40 percent of her blood supply as a result of internal bleeding. The blood loss triggered respiratory shock. Mrs. O'Neill was given a tracheotomy and was placed on a respirator for 24 days.

The accident had lasting consequences. It deprived Mrs. O'Neill of the ability to live life independently of others. It placed her into a nursing home, where she remains to this day.[22]

The plaintiff sued the driver and her insurance company. During settlement negotiations, the plaintiff's attorney asked for the policy limits of $20,000 (notwithstanding her medical bills, which amounted to $105,000, not including other damages) and offered a complete release from liability for the driver. The insurance company, however, refused to settle—despite its own attorneys urging it to do so. Almost a year later, while the trial was well under way, the insurance company offered the $20,000, but by then, the plaintiff thought it too late and refused the offer. A few days later, a jury awarded the plaintiff $731,063 in damages and $2.3 million in the form of punitive damages.

That verdict was the foundation for a subsequent bad-faith case against the insurer. The plaintiff presented 44 other cases against the insurer where Illinois customers suffered verdicts in excess of their policy limits after the insurer refused to settle within policy limits—to the tune of $10,849,313.

The court held:

> Where an insurer is pursued for its refusal to settle a claim, "bad faith" lies in an insurer's failure to give at least equal consideration to the insured's interest when the insurer

---

22. *Id.* at 1169.

arrives at a decision on whether to settle the claim. . . . This is precisely the standard set forth by [the] claims manager, when she wrote [the supervisor in charge of the decision] and gave her opinion of how Mrs. O'Neill's claim should be handled. She wrote that the policy limits should be tendered "in order to make sure that the policyholder's interests were treated with equal weight as the company's interests." Her admission, standing alone, provides ample evidence of bad faith. However, there was other evidence of bad faith to support the jury's verdict.[23]

Finally, there is a unique legal issue dealing with Halloween trick-or-treating, which, of course, is the single most important way of celebrating this holiday. The issue: Does the state, or a municipality, have the right to curtail registered sex offenders from handing out Halloween candy, or being present around small children during the holiday?

According to one Louisiana statute:

No person convicted of a sex offense, as defined in R.S.24:932, shall distribute candy or other gifts to persons under 18 years of age on or concerning Halloween, Mardi Gras, Easter, Christmas, or any other recognized holiday for which generally candy is distributed or other gifts given to persons under 18 years of age.[24]

In one Missouri case, sex offenders brought an action against state and county officials alleging that a similar yet even broader statute

---

23. *Id.* at 1172.
24. *See* 17 LA. CIV. CODE ANN. § 10:238 (database updated on Westlaw Dec. 2012).

October—Scary Cases: Halloween Pranks Gone Bad

violated various provisions of the United States Constitution and the Missouri Constitution.[25]

That statute provided:

> Any person required to register as a sexual offender under sections 589.400 to 589.425 shall be required on October thirty-first of each year to:
>
> 1. Avoid all Halloween-related contact with children;
> 2. Remain inside his or her residence between the hours of 5 p.m. and 10:30 p.m. unless required to be elsewhere for just cause, including but not limited to employment or medical emergencies;
> 3. Post a sign at his or her residence stating, "No candy or treats at this residence"; and
> 4. Leave all outside residential lighting off during the evening hours after 5 p.m.[26]

The sex offenders requested a preliminary injunction against enforcement of the statute, and the federal district court granted their request, but later dismissed the case as moot—in the meantime, the Missouri Supreme Court struck down the statute as unconstitutional, but applied it to a particular defendant whose conviction predated the statute. On appeal in the case brought by the defendants the circuit court affirmed, holding that the sex offenders' claims were moot.

> Considering the Missouri Supreme Court's decision, as well as the fact that each of the Does' obligation to register as

---

25. Doe v. Nixon, 2013 WL 1920790 (C.A. 8 (Mo. 2013)).
26. Mo. Rev. Stat. § 589.426.

a sex offender is derived from a conviction that predated the Halloween statute's enactment, we fail to see how any of the Officials could enforce the Halloween statute against the Does. This conclusion is bolstered by the lack of evidence that the Does are actually under a threat of arrest or prosecution.[27]

---

27. *Doe, supra* note 25, at 10.

October—Official State and Local Holidays

HAL-LAW-EEN WOULD BE REALLY SCARY!

Making the Plea for Candy into a Legal Holiday
Sean Carter

Copyright © 2005 American Bar Association[1]

A few nights ago, I engaged in an annual ritual that I find every bit as distasteful as the rubber chicken they serve at most bar functions. That annual ritual was the Running of the Masked Children, or, as you probably call it, Halloween.

I must confess that I just don't get the point of going door-to-door begging our neighbors for candy. As I see it, if we're going to humble ourselves to the point of begging for food (which, given my current occupation, is always a distinct possibility), then why not ask for something good?

I could get behind a holiday where you go door-to-door and yell, "Trick or treat! Trick or treat! Give me steak and lobster to eat!" I just don't see the point of walking a few miles for the promise of a Snickers bar, particularly when it requires me to buy several dozen bars to hand out to the beggars who will be ringing my doorbell all night.

My three boys, of course, see it differently. To them, Halloween is the most fun they can have without actually setting our house on fire. And why not? They aren't the ones who will be working into their mid-90s to pay off their dental bills. That honor and privilege will fall to me.

---

1. Sean Carter, *Hal-Law-Een Would Be Really Scary! Making the Plea for Candy into a Legal Holiday*, 4 A.B.A. J (2005).

The Little Book of Holiday Law

Holiday Humor (cont.)

For weeks leading up to the big day, I could hear them excitedly talking about it:

Austin: What are you going to be for Halloween? I'm going to be Darth Vader.

Matthew: Well, I'm going to be Spider-Man. What about you, Brendan?

Brendan: I'm going to be Mr. Incredible. What do you think Daddy's going to be?

Austin: Mad! That's what he was last year after the dentist said I had five cavities.

Of course, I can't really blame my boys. When I was a kid, I loved Halloween as well. In fact, the universal appeal of Halloween for children has given me another great idea to enhance the image of the legal profession. We need our own candy-giving holiday. Hal-*law*-een.

Think about it. Why should dentists be the only professionals to benefit from a children's holiday? Lawyers should also be able to benefit from the goodwill that comes from turning our children into panhandlers.

We could schedule the holiday on the eve of Law Day. Every April 30, children will wait until nightfall and then take to the streets dressed in blue and gray pin-striped suits and try to fill their briefcases with candy. They will be greeted at the front door by an adult dressed in a black robe, who will refuse to give the children any candy until they construct a valid legal argument to support their claim.

Child: We make our demand on this court for damages in the amount of one Baby Ruth bar and a pack of Bubble Yum.

Adult: On what grounds?

Child: On the grounds of detrimental reliance. We got dressed up in these ridiculous-looking clothes and trudged over to your

October—Official State and Local Holidays

house in reliance on the implied promise that you would give us free candy.

Adult: Do you have any precedent to support your theory of relief?

Child: Yes, Mr. Walters two doors down gave us candy.

Adult: OK, motion granted!

Now, I know you're thinking that Halloween isn't just about candy—it's about being scared silly. That's why Hal-*law*-een is such a great idea. What could be scarier than being a lawyer? As lawyers, we encounter some of the most frightful circumstances imaginable. In fact, some of them are just plain unimaginable, which explains how so many of us were "tricked" into becoming lawyers in the first place.

Sure, a haunted house can be scary, but it pales in comparison to your average courthouse. Let the children spend five minutes in a courthouse, and they'll be scared senseless (which, on second thought, probably isn't saying a lot). Just picture it:

After making it through the metal detectors, the children must submit their pleadings to a file clerk who is a stickler about the local rules. He yells at them, "I cannot accept these pleadings. They're stapled vertically in the upper left-hand corner! We require horizontal staples. Besides, there's no Bates stamping on your documents, and you wrote them in crayon. Next!"

They are then ushered into a courtroom and asked to make oral arguments before a particularly irritable and cranky judge, who substitutes her own lack of preparation with personal attacks.

"Well, little Suzy, if that's the best quantum meruit argument you can muster, I strongly suggest you contact your kindergarten for a refund!"

All the while, opposing counsel will scream that the children are completely unethical, unprofessional and incompetent and threaten to report them to the state bar. In the end, the court will

The Little Book of Holiday Law

strongly "encourage" each child to give up his claim of a bag full of candy in exchange for two Tic Tacs. I guarantee you that these children will run from the courthouse screaming. I know I always did.

Therefore, I suggest you get busy carving your Jack-o-Lectern, because Hal-*law*-een is just 177 days away. Tort or treat!

Chapter Eleven

November
A History of Blue Laws

"Blue" laws, or laws that mandate certain types of closings on Sundays, go far back in American history; as Chief Justice Warren of the U.S. Supreme Court once depicted in the case of *McGowan v. Maryland*, blue laws were brought to the colonies with a background of English legislation that dates to the 13th century.[1] In 1237, Henry III forbade the frequenting of markets on Sunday, and Henry IV prohibited the playing of unlawful games on the Lord's day, among other colonial prohibitions.[2] In fact, the law of the colonies in 1677 provided as follows:

> For the better observation and keeping holy the Lord's day, commonly called Sunday: be it enacted . . . that all the laws enacted and in force concerning the observation of the day, and repairing to the church thereon, be carefully put in execution; and that all and every person and persons whatsoever

---

1. *See* McGowan v. Maryland, 366 U.S. 420, at 432 (1961).
2. *Id.*

shall upon every Lord's day apply themselves to the observation of the same, by exercising themselves thereon in the duties of piety and true religion, publicly and privately; and that no tradesman, artificer, workman, laborer, or other person whatsoever, shall do or exercise any worldly labor or business or work of their ordinary callings upon the Lord's day, or any part thereof (works of necessity and charity only excepted); . . . and that no person or persons whatsoever shall publicly cry, show forth, or expose for sale any wares, merchandise, fruit, herbs, goods, chattels, whatsoever, upon the Lord's day, or any part thereof.[3]

Since colonial times, Sunday closing laws have enjoyed a long and embedded history in American law—they still exist today, in fact, in various forms and extents in many states and municipalities.[4] On May 29, 1961, the U.S. Supreme Court decided four notable cases regarding the constitutionality of blue laws.

Chief Justice Warren's opinion in *McGowan v. Maryland*, mentioned earlier, upheld a group of Maryland criminal statutes that provided for punishment for those who did not adhere to the mandatory Sunday closings proscribed by the state legislature. The case began when seven employees of a large discount department store were prosecuted for selling prohibited merchandise on a Sunday—namely, a three-ring loose-leaf binder, a can of floor wax, a stapler and staples, and a toy submarine.[5] The Sunday laws

---

3. *Id.*, citing to 29 Charles II, ch. 7.
4. *See, e.g.*: "Before the legislature abdicated its right to legislate in the field of Sunday closing laws, several Florida statutes authorized the imposition of sanctions for the conducting of certain businesses and trades on Sunday. One of these laws, prohibiting the taking of dead shrimp on Saturdays, Sundays, or legal state holidays, is still in effect." 49 FLA. JUR. 2D *Sundays and Holidays* § 7 (database updated on Westlaw Aug. 2013).
5. *Id.* at 422.

November—A History of Blue Laws

provided for a myriad of exemptions and immunities, allowing for recreational activities such as dancing, bowling, and amusement parks, along with the sale of merchandise that was customarily associated with the operation of those businesses and occupations offering said recreational activities. The statutes also provided for exceptions for necessities.

The appellants first argued that the Maryland Sunday laws violated the Equal Protection Clause of the Fourteenth Amendment, as the classifications contained in the statutes regarding which commodities may or may not be sold bore no rational relation to the object of the legislation. The Supreme Court disagreed:

> The standards under which this proposition is to be evaluated have been set forth many times by this Court. Although no precise formula has been developed, the Court has held that the Fourteenth Amendment permits the States a wide scope of discretion in enacting laws which affect some groups of citizens differently than others. The constitutional safeguard is offended only if the classification rests on grounds wholly irrelevant to the achievement of the state's objective. State legislatures are presumed to have acted within their constitutional power despite the fact that, in practice, their laws result in some inequality. A statutory discrimination will not be set aside if any statement of facts reasonably may be conceived to justify it.[6]

Applying those standards to the Sunday laws, the Court held that there was no indication that an apparently reasonable basis did not exist in Maryland's enacting of its Sunday laws, and that there was no evidence that the statutory distinctions were invidious.

---

6. McGowan, supra note 1 at 422.

> It would seem that a legislature could reasonably find that the Sunday sale of the exempted commodities was necessary either for the health of the populace or for the enhancement of the recreational atmosphere of the day that a family which takes a Sunday ride into the country will need gasoline for the automobile and may find pleasant a soft drink or fresh fruit; that those who go to the beach may wish ice cream or some other item normally sold there; that some people will prefer alcoholic beverages or games of chance to add to their relaxation; that newspapers and drug products should always be available to the public.[7]

The appellants further argued that the Sunday laws violated the Constitution's provisions for religious liberty. They argued, essentially, that the laws purposefully facilitated and encouraged Sunday church attendance and conduct, and that they therefore respected an establishment of religion generally and favored a particular religion specifically. The Court, as noted above, acknowledged that Sunday closing laws were steeped in religious history and tradition. However, it noted,

> nonreligious arguments for Sunday closing began to be heard more distinctly and the statutes began to lose some of their totally religious flavor. . . . More recently, further secular justifications have been advanced for making Sunday a day of rest, a day when people may recover from the labors of the week just passed and may physically and mentally prepare for the week's work to come.[8]

---

7. *Id.* at 426.
8. *Id.* at 433–34.

November—A History of Blue Laws

As an example, the Court cited to support for Sunday closing laws by labor groups and trade associations, upholding the Maryland statutes as constitutional.

In another case, the Court held that a Pennsylvania Sunday closing law was likewise constitutional.[9]

That statute provided:

> Whoever engages on Sunday in the business of selling, or offers for sale, on such day, at retail, clothing and wearing apparel, clothing accessories, furniture, housewares, home, business or office furnishings, household, business or office appliances, hardware, tools, paints, building and lumber supply materials, jewelry, silverware, watches, clocks, luggage, musical instruments and recordings, or toys, excluding novelties and souvenirs, shall, upon conviction thereof in a summary proceeding for the first offense, be sentenced to pay a fine of not exceeding one hundred dollars ($100), and for the second or any subsequent offense committed within one year after conviction for the first offense, be sentenced to pay a fine of not exceeding two hundred dollars ($200) or undergo imprisonment not exceeding thirty days in default thereof.[10]

As the Court noted, the Pennsylvania case looked much like the Maryland one: employees were prosecuted for violating the Sunday laws; there were exceptions for necessities and charity work, along with amendments allowing for recreational exemptions. The case involved a large discount department store business

---

9. Two Guys from Harrison-Allentown, Inc. v. McGinley, 366 U.S. 582 (1961).
10. *Id.* at 583, citing to 18 Purdon's PA. STAT. ANN. (1960 Cum. Supp.) § 4699.10.

that originated in New Jersey, where it experienced much success, and then expanded into Pennsylvania, where it sought to do business on Sundays as it did so in New Jersey. Several employees of the store were prosecuted under the Sunday closing laws of Pennsylvania.

The district court in the Pennsylvania case denied the appellants injunctive relief from enforcing the law, and the Supreme Court affirmed, holding that the legislature had reasonable purposes for treating certain businesses differently, and enacting the law that allowed for some activities but prohibited others. "It was within the power of the legislature to have concluded that these businesses were particularly disrupting the intended atmosphere of the day because of the great volume of motor traffic attracted, the danger of their competitors also opening on Sunday and their large number of employees," the Court noted.[11] "Of course, as to works of charity, necessity or recreation, the State Legislature could find that the interests of its citizens are best served by permitting these Sunday activities; that their interference with the absolute tranquility of the day is justified by their requirement and desirability."[12]

The same Pennsylvania statute was the subject of another Supreme Court decision, decided on the same day, but this time involving an additional issue: Does the statute violate the Constitution's Free Exercise Clause when applied to a group that practices a different religion, one whose day of repose falls on a day other than Sunday?

Braunfeld v. Brown involved a lawsuit brought by Orthodox Jewish merchants in Philadelphia who engaged in the sale of retail clothing and merchandise and wished to remain open on Sundays.[13]

---

11. *Id.* at 591.
12. *Id.* at 590.
13. Braunfeld v. Brown, 366 U.S. 599 (1961).

November—A History of Blue Laws

The merchants argued that because their religion requires them to remain closed on the Sabbath—from sundown on Friday to sundown on Saturday—they are seriously disadvantaged economically when they also have to remain closed on Sundays. The merchants argued that "this result will either compel appellants to give up their Sabbath observance, a basic tenet of the Orthodox Jewish faith, or will put appellants at a serious economic disadvantage if they continue to adhere to their Sabbath."[14]

While recognizing that adhering to the statute will result in some sacrifice by the appellants, the Court did not see a violation of the Free Exercise Clause, and instead held that there was merely an incidental burden on the practice of religion. "To strike down, without the most critical scrutiny, legislation which imposes only an indirect burden on the exercise of religion, i.e. legislation which does not make unlawful the religious practice itself, would radically restrict the operating latitude of the legislature," the Court noted, citing such examples as statutes that tax and limit deductions for religious contributions, and court closings on Saturdays and Sundays.[15]

> [W]e are a cosmopolitan nation made up of people of almost every conceivable religious preference. These denominations number almost three hundred. . . . Consequently, it cannot be expected, much less required, that legislators enact no law regulating conduct that may in some way result in an economic disadvantage to some religious sects and not to others because of the special practices of the various religions. We do not believe that such an effect is an absolute test

---

14. *Id.* at 602.
15. *Id.* at 606.

for determining whether the legislation violates the freedom of religion protected by the First Amendment.[16]

In the last of the four cases decided that day, the Supreme Court also upheld the Massachusetts Sunday closing laws. Involving a kosher supermarket, its Orthodox Jewish customers, and the rabbis who worked to certify meat as kosher for sale in the market, the parties challenged the laws (which prohibited most business on Sundays but provided for several exemptions for charity, necessities, and recreation) on the same grounds as above. The Court compared the case to the cases discussed earlier involving Maryland and Pennsylvania laws and upheld the Massachusetts statutes.[17]

---

16. *Id.* at 606–07.
17. Gallagher v. Crown Kosher Super Market of Massachusetts, Inc., 366 U.S. 617 (1961).

November—A History of Blue Laws

New and not-so-new lawyers alike will find the following a funny (albeit accurate) account of the holidays for newbies; it originally appeared in the *ABA Journal*.

AT THE FIRM FOR THE HOLIDAYS

These Helpful Hints Will Help You Celebrate While You Work

The Rodent

Copyright © 2002 American Bar Association; The Rodent[1]

If you're a new lawyer, you should know that this Christmas will be different from the ones you enjoyed before you started walking around with a bar card in your wallet. While partners at The Firm are running off to vacation at some winter wonderland even though there is work to do, it's not hard to figure out who will be left behind trying to meet those year-end deadlines. That will be you.

This scenario has created some of the most memorable tales of associate Christmases past. One commonly shared memory is the experience of having to work late, missing a flight and ending up spending Christmas Eve on a cold airport floor.

Another memorable seasonal story is the one of the associate who tried to deliver documents to a partner's vacation home during a blizzard. His car skidded off the road, and he spent at least a couple of the 12 days of Christmas trapped in a snow bank. Adding insult to injury, lawyers in these situations can usually only bill

---

1. *At The Firm for the Holidays, These Helpful Hints Will Help You Celebrate While You Work*, 1 ABA J. (2002).

The Little Book of Holiday Law

clients for the time they spend in the snow bank, as clients tend to balk at paying for time spent in a hospital being treated for frostbite.

Such experiences teach attorneys the true meaning of a law firm Christmas. They also make lawyers appreciate the relative comfort and safety of spending the holidays at the office. It's better simply to make plans to be at The Firm rather than make plans you will never be able to keep.

But don't despair! Instead, do what you can to make the best of the situation. Here are some helpful holiday hints and thoughts to cheer you up:

- If you drive to work, traffic on Christmas morning is certain to be far lighter than usual. Give yourself a special holiday treat by sleeping an extra 10 minutes before going to the office.
- The Firm computer is likely to have a faster Internet connection than your home computer. This will reduce the time it takes to send electronic Christmas cards to all the people who are so important to you.
- Buy yourself a present on the way to the office (7-Eleven is open 24 hours, even on Christmas) and unwrap it at your desk while waiting for documents to be proofread.
- Bring a cassette tape of Christmas carols and play them on your dictaphone.
- In lieu of going to church with loved ones, gather with other associates for services in the senior partner's office.
- Come to the office dressed as your favorite biblical character.
- Use a fire extinguisher to make your office part of a white Christmas.
- Call home while the family is gathered around the fire opening presents, and listen to them on your speakerphone while you do your work.

November—A History of Blue Laws

- Don't forget to think of the less fortunate on this special day. Specifically, remember that while you may not yet be a partner, there are those who rank even lower than you on the law firm totem pole. Take advantage of your senior position and keep from getting lonely by making a first-year associate and a paralegal or two come to the office and share in The Firm festivities.

If these steps fail to make your holiday a joyous occasion, it's probably because being at The Firm has caused your post-Christmas depression to kick in early this year. The good news is that you might also get over it earlier than usual and actually feel like celebrating on New Year's Eve.

That is, of course, assuming you don't have to work that night. Merry Christmas and Happy New Fiscal Year!

Chapter Twelve

December
Holiday Party Liability: Cases on Social Host Liability, Office Party Suits, and More

Most companies love to throw a good party for their employees—whether it's to increase camaraderie, convey a sense of appreciation, take stock in the employer's progress through the year, or just get together to celebrate something good.

As one author writes:

> [W]hile there are many good reasons to throw a holiday party for your customers and employees, surprising antics can occur as the office team relaxes at the event. Take, for instance, the corporate executive who mooned his staff, much to their dismay. No buts about it—that just wasn't a good act. We caution you to make sure your happy events don't become a breeding ground for two specific legal liabilities: sexual harassment and DUI-related accidents.[1]

---

1. Jennifer S. Kessler, *Ho! Ho! Uh-Oh! The Perils of Office Holiday Parties, in* 19 Virginia Employment Law Letter 1 (2007).

The author goes on to note that many sexual harassment suits are the result of advances at office parties between coworkers, and cites to a Lawyers.com survey sponsored by LexisNexis, according to which "29 percent of adults have observed or experienced sexual advances at office parties between people who work together."[2]

To help avoid sexual harassment lawsuits, the author provides the following tips:

> Beware of employees engaged in inappropriate touching. A single incident can be an actionable event under Title VII of the Civil Rights Act of 1964 if it's serious enough.
>
> Watch the behavior between your employees and any clients or customers. If a client makes an inappropriate advance toward an employee, your company may be liable, particularly if the employee feels pressured to make the client "comfortable" or "happy" and acquiesces to his demands.
>
> You need to watch both men and women. In [one] case, a male employee filed a sexual harassment claim in federal court after his female supervisor harassed him at two holiday parties. At the first party, the supervisor attempted to kiss the employee under the mistletoe and force him to dance with her. She commented, "[I]f it was this difficult to get you on the dance floor, how difficult would it be for me to take you home?" At the second party, she followed him around, making suggestive faces, the entire evening.
>
> How spouses and guests of your employees are treated is also your concern, albeit not necessarily from a legal standpoint. Even though an employee's spouse can't sue the company for harassment, the fact that the incident occurred

---

2. *Id.*

December—Holiday Party Liability

at an office party can cause problems in the workplace from friction between the employees involved.[3]

Then there is the issue of liability for the acts of employees. Even though a party host may not be liable for the behavior of a guest, as an employer, you may be liable for the behavior of an employee who is acting within the scope of his employment, the author warns.

Whether attending a company holiday party is "within the scope of employment" varies on a case-by-case basis. If attendance is mandatory, a court will probably find employees to be acting within the scope of their employment. If attendance isn't technically mandatory but there's a strong expectation that all employees will or should attend, a court may infer that attendance was expected and thus find employees to be acting within the scope of their employment.[4]

In addition, the courts might consider whether the party was held at the employer's workplace premises, and whether it was during work hours. If the injuries result from the actions of an inebriated employee, the court will also consider whether drinking was a part of the employee's work duties. "If a court determines that attendance at the holiday party was within the scope of an employee's employment, then it will most likely hold the employer vicariously liable for the actions of an inebriated employee."[5]

3. *Id.*
4. *Id.*
5. *Id.*

> ### Holiday Fast Facts—New Year's Eve
>
> Originally, the owners of Times Square held rooftop celebrations. In 1907, the ball was dropped for the first time. Back then, the ball was made of iron and wood, and decorated with 100 light bulbs; contrast that with the 2001 ball, which was made of Waterford crystal and decorated by 600 bulbs.[1]
>
> ---
>
> 1. JIM MCCANN & JEANNE BENEDICT, CELEBRATIONS: A JOYOUS GUIDE TO HOLIDAYS FROM PAST TO PRESENT 144 (2001).

The author cites to two Virginia cases. In the first, an employer hosted an office holiday party on its premises, and two employees drank at the party until they became intoxicated. After leaving in separate cars, the two employees collided and injured a passenger, who filed a negligence claim against the employer. The court held that while the employer wasn't liable under the theory of social host liability, it was potentially liable under respondeat superior.[6] In the second case, an employee was struck and killed by another employee while leaving an office holiday party. Though attendance at the party technically wasn't mandatory, the employer permitted its workers to leave early the day of the party and strongly encouraged employees to attend with their families; attendance was almost universal. Applying respondeat superior, the court found the employer liable, holding that the party was closely connected and associated with employment.[7]

---

6. *Id.*, citing to *Sayles v. Ford Motor Co.*
7. *Id.*, citing to *Kim v. Sportswear.*

December—Holiday Party Liability

Some courts have declined to hold employers responsible in these situations. In one Wisconsin case, a manager and coworker attended a company-sponsored holiday party. The coworker became intoxicated, and the bartender asked him if he had a ride home. Overhearing the conversation, the manager agreed to drive him home, but he left the party without the coworker. The coworker attempted to drive home, crossed into oncoming traffic, and was killed along with the driver of another vehicle. That driver's estate sued the manager and the company.

The lower courts found that the manager had volunteered to take the intoxicated coworker home, and that a jury could reasonably infer that the manager was negligent in leaving the coworker at the party. In a separate decision, the appeals court held that the employer could be held responsible if the manager acted within the scope of his duties when he agreed to drive the coworker home.

The Wisconsin Supreme Court disagreed, however, refusing to hold the manager liable based on public policy factors. "The court found that the injuries sustained in the case were completely out of proportion to any wrongdoing by [the manager]," explains an article detailing the case. "It also concluded that to allow him to be potentially liable for damages under the circumstances of the case would allow the law to enter a field that has no sensible or just stopping point."[8]

There is a special problem with alcohol at company parties: the problem of underage employees or guests. "They're called 'adult' beverages for a good reason," notes one author. "Is your company planning to have a holiday party for employees and their guests? If so, you'd better know the age of all in attendance and take precautions to ensure that no one underage drinks alcoholic beverages."[9]

---

8. Michael J. Modi, *Broken Promises: Wisconsin Supreme Court Decides Holiday Party Case, in* 11 WISCONSIN EMPLOYMENT LAW LETTER 1 (2002).
9. Gayla McSwain, *The Holiday Party—Beware, in* 16 SOUTH CAROLINA

The Little Book of Holiday Law

Some states will hold the employer liable for injuries suffered as a result of underage drinking. As an example, the aforementioned author cites to two South Carolina cases: the first one involved a holiday cookout for business acquaintances at the home of an employee, at which a 19-year-old was allowed to drink alcohol, then was later killed in a single-car accident while driving home; the second involved another 19-year-old guest at a work-related holiday party who was served alcohol by the bartender and was killed in a two-car accident while driving home.

The article offers some helpful suggestions to control the serving of alcoholic beverages during company-sponsored parties:

- Limit the number of drinks served by requiring tickets or some other means to limit access.
- Before the function, encourage the use of designated drivers.
- Serve plenty of food.
- Think about limiting the length of the function because the longer people are at a party, the greater the chance for them to drink more.
- Always consider having alternative transportation available so that each person who attends has a safe way home at the end of the function.[10]

EMPLOYMENT LAW LETTER 1 (2007).
   10. *Id.*

A LITTLE HUMOR: HOLIDAY OFFICE PARTY SUGGESTIONS—NOT!

Christopher McFadden[1]

A holiday office party is a time to kick back, relax, and say, "Thanks for a great year of hard work!" But that doesn't mean it can't be an opportunity to keep learning! HR professionals know that it never hurts to reinforce important lessons about appropriate workplace conduct, whatever the setting. With that in mind, we present a little holiday humor. (If you start saying to yourself as you read this, "That's a really good idea," you can't blame us when it backfires on you!)

No "hostile environment" without a "host"

Remember, it's called a holiday party—even if it's in the office. So be a good host! Host an event that people are excited to attend. Provide some good food and fun activities. Then, after you get them in the door, hit 'em with some employment training through themed activities. Here are some ideas.

Title VII layer cake. Serving this multicolored delectable dish of diversity will remind employees of the requirements of Title VII—it's not OK to discriminate on the basis of race, color, religion, sex, or national origin. For those who miss that message, at least it will be tasty.

On a serious note, it is quite possible that sexual orientation will become a sixth protected category soon, as proposed legislation

---

1. 15 Arizona Employment Law Letter 5 (2008).

The Little Book of Holiday Law

to add that category to Title VII appears to have enough support in Congress. We'll keep you posted.

Lemon-ADEA. When your confused employee asks why a traditional summer drink like lemonade is appearing alongside eggnog at your winter holiday party, use it as an opportunity to explain that drinks are like people—some are May, and some are December, but they're all OK in your book year-round! Add some Russian vodka to the lemonade to reinforce national origin discrimination. (OK, don't even think about it.)

Kidding aside, under the Age Discrimination in Employment Act (ADEA), 40 is the magic number. If an employee is over 40, you cannot take employment action against her because of her age. Also, in this economic environment, layoffs have become more common, and employees over 40 have certain rights under those circumstances as well. To be on the safe side, consult with your employment attorney before conducting a layoff.

Forty-yard ADOSH. No holiday party is complete without fun games and contests. Remind employees about the Arizona Division of Occupational Safety and Health (ADOSH) Act by having them run around a maze of candy canes in the dark. Employees recognizing the activity as a violation of the ADOSH Act win a prize! Those who don't may still learn important lessons about workers' comp.

OK, so we're obviously not serious about running a race in the dark. But you should always be serious about workplace safety. Under ARS § 23–403(A), you have a general duty to provide a workplace that is free from recognized hazards that could cause serious harm. Federal laws provide similar protection.

Hot-stEPPA dance contest. Employees don't like lie detector tests—at least that's the case if you believe them. But they do love dance contests. Teach employees about the Employee Polygraph Protection Act (EPPA) with an interpretive dance contest in which

December—Holiday Party Liability

one team is "lies" and the other is "truth." You have to guess which team is which without the benefit of a polygraph. Bonus points for individuals who do a dance interpretation of those squiggly lines on the polygraph test. But remember, if the police administer a polygraph, that's not a violation of the Act, so make sure you have someone suddenly pop out of a cake in full police gear to drive that point home.

All right, so the polygraph dance might not be such a great idea. But remember, among other things, the EPPA prevents certain employers from requiring, requesting, suggesting, or causing any employee or prospective employee to take a lie detector test.

Bottom line

Holiday parties carry their own set of risks for employment claims, and we certainly advise you to discuss with your employment counsel what those risks may be depending on the type of party you intend to throw. In any event, we wish you all a great holiday season!

Index

A

ACLU of New Jersey v. Schundler (1999), 11
Adams, John, 72
Adams, Sherman, 52–53
Age Discrimination in Employment Act (ADEA), 124
American Civil Liberties Union (ACLU), 6

B

Bank holidays, 84
Blue Laws, 105–107
Bush, Prescott, 48
Business filings and transactions deadlines, 77–78, 83–85

C

Cammack v. Waihee (1991), 39–41
Centennial Exposition, 74
Child custody and visitation issues during holidays, 25–26
Christmas Day, 81, 82, 113–114
Christmas trees, 13
Citizenship Day, 82
Civil Rights Act of 1964. *See* Title VII protections
Columbus Day, 81
Commemorative days, 84

Communists and May Day celebrations, 47
Computation of time
  for business filings and transactions, 77–78
  for legal proceedings, 71–72
Constitution Day, 82
Constitution Week, 82
Content-based prior restraint, 20
County of Allegheny v. ACLU, Greater Pittsburgh Chapter (1989), 8–10
Court proceedings, Sunday prohibition on, 69–71
Crèche displays, 6, 8, 9–10, 11
Criminal cases based on Halloween pranks and mischief, 87–89
Custody issues involving holidays, 25–26
Cyclopedia of Federal Procedure, 81

D

Deadlines
  for business filings and transactions, 77–78
  for legal proceedings, 71–72

Index

Discrimination on religious grounds, 59–60
DUI-related accidents, 117, 119, 120–122
Dulles, John Foster, 48

E
Eid Al-Fitr and Eid Al-Adha, 63
Eisenhower, Dwight D., 50, 51, 52–53
Employee Polygraph Protection Act (EPPA), 124
Employers
    holiday parties, 117–118, 123–124
    religious discrimination, 59–60
English Blue Laws, 105–107
Equal Employment Opportunity Commission (EEOC), 61
Equal Protection Clause, 107
Establishment Clause, 4–5, 6, 8, 10, 15, 39–41, 41

F
Father's Day, 51
Federal Rules of Civil Procedure, 73
First Amendment
    Establishment Clause, 4–5, 6, 8, 10, 15, 39–41, 41
    Free Exercise Clause, 4–5, 111
Forum classification
    designated public forum, 5
    limited public forum, 5
    nonpublic forum, 6
    traditional public forum, 5
Fourteenth Amendment, 17, 107–108
Fourth of July, 72, 74, 81
Free Exercise Clause, 4–5, 111
Free speech protection. *See* First Amendment

G
Good Friday, 39–41, 82
Government filings, holiday extensions for, 77–78

H
Halloween, 18–19, 60–62
    holiday humor, 99–100
    pranks and mischief, 87–89
    sex offenders' participation in, 96–97
Henry III, 105
Henry IV, 105
Holiday humor, 43–44, 51, 54, 99–100, 113–114
Holiday parties, 117–118, 123–124
Holidays. *See also* Religious holidays
    bank holidays, 84
    in computation of time for legal proceedings, 71–72

Index

lawyers working on, 113–114
legal holidays, 81–82
personal holidays, 84
Hostile work environment, 60, 123

I
Independence Day. *See* Fourth of July
International Audit Month, 51
International Men's Month, 51

J
JDSupra.com, 43
Jefferson, Thomas, 72
Judicial holidays, 69–71, 83
July fourth. *See* Fourth of July

K
Kuwait, 62

L
Labor Day, 81
Law Day, 47–49, 55
Lawyers working on holidays, 113–114
Leases, termination falling on Sunday or holiday, 78
Legal holidays, 81–82
Lemon test, 4, 17
Loyalty Day, 47
Lynch v. Donnelly (1984), 6–7, 11

M
Martin Luther King Jr.'s Birthday, 81
May Day, 47
McGowan v. Maryland (1961), 105, 106–108
Memorial Day, 81
Metzl v. Leininger (1995), 40, 42
Monroe, James, 72
Mother's Day, 51

N
National Barbeque Month, 51
National Bathroom Reading Month, 51
National Camping Month, 51
National Meditation Month, 51
National Smile Month, 51
Negligence cases based on Halloween pranks and mischief, 92–93
Negotiable instruments payable on Sunday or holiday, 78–79
New Year's Day, 81
New Year's Eve, 120
New York ban on service of process on Sundays and holidays, 70
Nonpublic forum, 6

O
O'Connor, Sandra Day, 10–11

Index

Official holidays, 81–82

P

Parks as traditional public fora, 5
Personal holidays, 84
Personal injury cases based on Halloween pranks and mischief, 92–93
Pielech v. Massasoit Greyhound, Inc. (1996), 59
Prayers in schools, 15
Presidents' Day, 18
Prior restraint, 20
Public displays of religious holiday items, 3–4. *See also* Crèche displays
Public forum
    designated, 5
    free speech rights in, 4
    holiday displays on, 14
    limited, 5
    nonpublic forum, 6
    traditional, 5

R

Reasonable accommodation, 65, 66
Religious discrimination, 59–60
Religious holiday items
    in workplace, 65
    public display of, 3–4. *See also* Crèche displays

Religious holidays designated as legal holidays, 82
Retail businesses and Blue Laws, 105–107
Rhyne, Charles, 48, 51–52, 53
Rule of Law, 49–51
Rule of Sequestration, 88
Russian May Day strikes, 47

S

Saturday
    business filing or transaction deadlines on, 78–79
    half-holiday, 83
    in computation of time for legal proceedings, 71–72
    judicial holidays including, 83
Saudi Arabia, 63–64
School board meeting rooms, 5
School holiday displays, 13–15
School prayer, 15
School vacations, holidays falling during, 25
Separation of church and state, 3, 6
Sequestration Rule, 88
Service of process on Sundays and holidays, 70
Sex offenders, Halloween participation of, 96–97
Sexual harassment, 117–118

Index

Sidewalks as traditional public fora, 5
State college classrooms, 5
St. Patrick's Day, 36
Streets as traditional public fora, 5
Strict scrutiny analysis, 4
Sunday. *See also* Blue Laws
 business filings and transactions deadlines on, 77–78
 in computation of time for legal proceedings, 71–72
 legal proceedings on, 69–71

T
Thanksgiving Day, 81
 Friday after, 72–73
Title VII protections, 63, 118, 123

U
Uncle Sam image, 74
Undue hardship, 65, 66
Uniform Negotiable Instruments Law, 79

V
Valentine's Day, 9
Veterans' Day, 81
Vicarious liability, 119–121
Visitation issues involving holidays, 25–26

W
Washington's Birthday, 81
Workplace holiday parties, 117–118, 123–124
Workplace religious discrimination, 59–60
Workplace safety, 124–125

About the Author

Ursula Furi-Perry is the author of ten other books:

- *50 Legal Careers for Non-Attorneys* (ABA Publishing 2008)
- *50 Unique Legal Paths: How to Find the Right Job* (ABA Publishing 2008)
- *Law School Revealed: Secrets, Opportunities and Success!* (Jist Publishing 2009)
- *Trial Prep for Paralegals* (National Institute for Trial Advocacy 2009) (coauthor)
- *Your First Year as a Lawyer Revealed* (Jist Publishing 2010)
- *The Legal Assistant's Complete Desk Reference* (ABA Publishing 2011 and 2013)
- *Trial Prep for the New Advocate* (LexisNexis via National Institute for Trial Advocacy 2011) (coauthor)
- *The Millennial Lawyer: Making the Most of Generational Differences in the Firm* (ABA Publishing 2012)
- *The Little Book of Fashion Law* (ABA Publishing 2013)
- *Constitutional Law for Kids* (ABA Publishing 2013)

Furi-Perry has also published more than 300 articles in national and regional publications, including Law.com, American Lawyer Media, *Legal Assistant Today, PreLaw Magazine, National Jurist,* and LawCrossing.com.

Furi-Perry is director of Academic Support and director of Bar Essay Writing at the Massachusetts School of Law at Andover. She received her juris doctor, magna cum laude, from the Massachusetts School of Law. She is a partner in the firm of Dill & Furi-Perry, LLP, in Haverhill, Massachusetts.